Contents

Acknowledgements ix

Preface 1

1. Straw Sticking in my Bum 5

2. Floods of Tears 40

3. Dead Man's Bay 62

4. Australia Bound 87

5. Indecent Exposure 113

6. The Scum of the Earth 144

7. A Change of Direction 164

8. The Law of Averages 187

9. School Report 210

10. Dole to Doctorate 240

11. Chance Happenings 266

12. Be Kind to Books 287

    Epilogue 312

ACKNOWLEDGEMENTS

Special thanks are due to several people and organisations that have made a contribution to this book:

Firstly my wife, Olivia: she is always the first person to read my work, and she is constructive and encouraging at all times. She is also the one who shares my long periods of isolation while working on a book.

Alfred Price for use of the image of a doodlebug.

The National Maritime Museum and the Museum of London: for permission to use historic photos of Tilbury Docks and women hop picking.

Maureen Reeve, Lisa Chapman, and Josephine Massey: for permission to reproduce family photos.

Geoff Barsby: for allowing the use of some of his valuable photos related to the floods of 1953.

Barbara Carter: who rationalised the many and varied formats of the ancient photos into a single method of presentation.

Nicola Guy and Richard Saunders: my editors at The History Press, who made the final stages of the completion of this book a most enjoyable and painless experience.

And, lastly, the many good people of Essex who shared with me their experience of the war years, hop picking, and the floods of 1953.

PREFACE

Through *Hops, Doodlebugs and Floods*, I have tried to create a funny, thought-provoking book. It begins with my early childhood as part of a typical East End of London family during the bygone age of the Second World War, and the evacuation of my family out into the relative peace of Essex; I became an "Essex Boy".

Like many ex-London families, we continued our annual exodus from Essex to go hop picking in Kent, even during the war years. Although we picked hops while the war in the air raged above us, there was still much humour that I have related.

My school life seemed blighted by my failure to pass the infamous Eleven-Plus examination, after which it was many years before I put that demon to rest. It was during my school years that I experienced the devastating east coast floods of 1953, during which some of my school friends and their family members lost their lives, but even during that sad event British humour and resolution shone through.

In 1956, I joined the Merchant Navy, illegally at the age of fifteen (through a clerical error!). I spent five years as a seaman and this time broadened my horizons as I grew from a boy to a man. I experienced a brush with danger getting caught up in the Suez War, suffered appendicitis while sailing down the coast of Africa and spent a brief spell in jail in Australia, all at the tender age of fifteen. My service in the Merchant Navy also brought me into contact with British people immigrating to Australia for the princely sum of £10. My memories of my five years as a seaman are full of excitement and all the fun that teenage years should contain.

The need for medical attention for hearing problems led me to a life "on land". I relate here the trials of soul destroying long-term unemployment that eventually inspired me to take on the long slog from limited learning to academic excellence and personal security, with a dizzy rise from life on the dole to a doctorate in just sixteen years.

My meteoric academic development, once it took off, opened a whole new world of career opportunities, including five years at management level with a multinational company, and a long, enjoyable time as a teacher in Essex. This was followed by a satisfying period as a practising psychologist. The spectre of failure and unemployment was finally put to rest!

My entry into the world of publishing was just one result of an amazing number of coincidences that has influenced my personal development. This is my thirty-first book, and my first non-academic publication.

Although this book largely describes my own experiences, I have tried to ensure that you will not be overwhelmed with my personal history. In writing the book my aim was to convey a thought-provoking memoir laced with humour, and a chronicle of what was taking place in Essex at that time.

I hope that you will recognise the trials and progress of a life that you can relate to. We all face tough times in our lives. Hopefully, at such difficult or despairing moments you will be inspired by the trials and difficulties I have overcome, and be inspired by my achievements. Most of all, I hope that you will be thoroughly amused throughout the book.

CHAPTER ONE

STRAW STICKING IN MY BUM

I was born on 24 December 1940. I have tried to practice walking on water ever since, but my family still accuse me of trying to ruin every Christmas since my momentous entry into the world in the middle of an air raid on London during the Blitz. On the way to the hospital, my father had to abandon buses twice because they were hit by enemy incendiary flares, perhaps a forewarning of what my entry into the world implied.

I was born into a typical close-knit extended family of the East End of war-torn London. I didn't have any say in the matter, it just happened. The family relationship was so close, that I grew up not fully comprehending the difference in the relationship between one set of grandparents and the other. They seemed intermingled. Many family activities such as parties, or even moving home, involved many of the extended family.

As a family, we gradually left London during the Blitz of the Second World War, and settled on Canvey Island, in the relative peace of the estuary of the River

Thames; I became an "Essex Boy". Some of my aunts and uncles were just a little older than me, and later I was to be in school with them, so it was difficult to view them as aunts and uncles in the accepted sense that is more common today. I became particularly close to two of these young aunts.

One of my earliest memories of life outside of London was watching my father and neighbours creating our Anderson air raid shelter. First an oblong trench was dug. How I yearned to get among that lovely mud! Six steel sheets were inserted into the two widest sides of the trench and bolted together at the top, to form a curved tunnel. The shaped ends were bolted in position, one of which had an opening for the door.

It was at this stage I experienced my first entry to the shelter. It was dark and smelled of damp earth. The next day all the earth that had been dug out of the trench was piled over the sides and the top of the shelter. We were now supposed to be ready to meet the might of the German bombers.

One of the other distinct wartime memories I have as a kid happened in the bungalow we lived in on Canvey Island. I remember hearing a strange buzzing noise that got louder and louder. Then it suddenly stopped and my mum, who was in the room with me, let out a piercing scream and grabbed hold of me tightly. Then, there was a terrific bang. I saw my sister's pram that was close to the window literally bounce in the air, with her in it. Fortunately, the window didn't break and shower her with glass.

I was only young during the war years but this incident left its mark on my memory. It was my first experience of a "doodlebug", or flying bomb. It had crashed and exploded not far from our house. Later I became a school friend of one of those injured who survived the blast.

Apart from the memory of the doodlebug hit, there are other wartime experiences that disturb me to this day. One example of this is the sound of an air-raid siren that always makes my stomach turn. After the war, the old air-raid siren continued to be used on Canvey to summon the volunteer fire brigade, or to warn of the danger of flooding. Today, periodically, the siren is tested and is still used to warn of flooding, and it never fails to affect me.

I can recall my mum taking me out into the garden late one night to show me the "pretty lights" in the sky. These were aircraft tracer bullets and anti-aircraft fire. Perhaps she felt I should be rewarded for arriving ignominiously on Christmas Eve and spoiling the family Christmas, not that there was a lot to celebrate that year.

During the war we had a lovely rag-bag of a dog called Prince. He was good company for my Mum and I while my Dad was on Home Guard duties at night. When the bombers thundered overhead causing my Mum and me to quiver in fear, Prince was completely relaxed. However, strangely, he trembled in terror when there was a thunderstorm, which is something that has always thrilled me.

Prince was an Old English Sheepdog, a gentle loveable animal with a will to please. I loved him at first sight, and he, as dogs do, returned my love completely. He followed me everywhere and I soon taught him to do many things. I started by getting him to stay while I walked some way, and only to come when I called him to my side. In due course I taught him to stay while I disappeared from view, and then come and find me, usually on top of the air-raid shelter. But his greatest accomplishment was in playing hide-and-seek. Unlike my other play friends he never tired of being the seeker, although he had the considerable advantage of his sensitive nose.

Some of my earliest and most enjoyable childhood memories are from the hop picking fields of Kent where I was initiated into the traditional "holiday" of London's East Enders during the war years, and after our move to Canvey Island, we continued the annual migration of Londoners to the Kent hop fields each September. These "holidays" lasted for about four weeks. It has been estimated that the numbers of migrant hop pickers was as high as 100,000 at times.

During the war years there was an absence of men folk who were engaged in war work. Hop picking, or "hopping" as it was usually called, provided a useful contribution to the family income, as well as giving a kind of working holiday. This was the only kind of holiday that many of us could hope for in those days. Not that it could really be called a holiday. Hop picking was backbreaking and messy work, and involved many hardships. But for many ex-hop pickers it is viewed with a sense of nostalgia.

Families would write away to the farms asking for work in the next hop picking season. In due course they would receive their "first" letter, guaranteeing them a place for the next season. Usually families would return to the same farm year after year, and often they would be re-allocated the same hut as accommodation. Sometimes families who were regulars at the same farm would visit "their" hut during the summer before the season started to make it more habitable. The arrival of the "second" letter from the farmer was the signal to join the farm promptly because harvesting was imminent.

Throughout the year, old clothes that would normally have been discarded were collected in the "hopping box". This was a large trunk or tea chest, and it was the repository of the strangest combination of fashion wear. You always wore old clothes while hop picking as they got so stained and smelly from the hops. My pride of attire from the hopping box during my early teens was a pair of horse riding jodhpurs. These were perfect for hiding the ill-gotten gains of a scrumping expedition into the orchards that adjoined the hop fields. Wellie boots were essential footwear for working in the fields and they were worn for most of the hopping season.

During the year food, such as tea, tins of corned beef, and other goodies, would also be saved and packed in the "hopping box", along with blankets and pillows. All necessary cooking utensils would also have to be made ready. Anything that it was thought might come in handy would be packed ready for the mass exodus to Kent.

Prior to the start of the hopping season the hopping boxes would be sent ahead to the farms. They were either forwarded by rail to be collected at the destination station by the farmer, or a lorry driver would be enticed to make a diversion during journeys for their employer. In Kent, the fields where the hops were grown were often referred to as hop "gardens". They were certainly the only gardens many Londoners experienced.

The excitement mounted among the children of hop pickers as the time approached to leave for the hop fields at the end of August for the September season. Sometimes the picking period could extend into October, depending on the weather. This excitement was not only in anticipation of a glorious four weeks holiday, but also in the knowledge that we would miss a further four weeks of schooling following the long school summer holiday. For some families the hop picking season was also followed by fruit picking.

Eventually the time to depart would arrive and the mass migration of hop pickers from their home towns would begin, in my case from Canvey Island. The journey to the hop fields would be undertaken by a variety of means of transport, sometimes with whole families on an open-backed lorry. Fat people were levered on board with much laughter. Old people were perched perilously on collapsible chairs and wrapped in blankets. Lorry journeys involved an exciting crossing of the Thames via the ferry at Tilbury or Woolwich, or the mysterious Blackwall Tunnel. In later years, due to new traffic acts, hoppers were no longer allowed to ride on the backs of lorries and more conventional transport had to be used.

My favourite way of reaching the hop fields was to go by train. For us, it meant travelling into badly war-damaged London to catch the train into wildest Kent. On the journey into London, barrage balloons could be seen, like huge tethered silver whales, floating high above the railway stations, and dotted in the sky along the route into the Kent countryside. Men in the stirring uniforms of the different services were seen everywhere, much to the wonder of children travellers.

The "'Oppers Special" was invariably a ramshackle train that appeared to have been brought out of mothballs just to carry the hoppers into what we looked on as the wild countryside. This left London Bridge Station in the early hours of the morning on the way to our destination in Kent. The particular train we caught was referred to as "Puffing Billy", but I am sure that was not the real name of it.

Bulky boxes and chests were loaded into the luggage wagon at the rear of the train. In spite of this, all kinds of strange shaped packages were jammed into the carriages, wedged into the luggage racks or supported on laps. The strangest "luggage" I saw in a carriage was a huge lady with a voluminous skirt, from which emerged a little lad like myself who had been made to hide to avoid paying a fare.

11

Some children, who were older than me, described how they would get past the ticket collector by rushing by and shouting out, "Mum's got my ticket." All clever stuff, or so it seemed to me!

On one journey to the hop fields I remember a woman putting her two young children up in the luggage rack, where they slept soundly. I thought this would be an exciting adventure but I was not allowed to achieve such dizzy heights.

It only took a little while for the hoppers to get comfortable for what in those days was a long journey ahead. There were friends from previous seasons to update on events that had taken place over the past year, and new friends to make. During the journey picnics would be unpacked and shared around the carriage. Some of the "posh" people even had thermos flasks!

After a while isolated sing-songs developed throughout the train. These would include current popular songs, as well as ones that belonged to the hoppers. They would improvise from time to time to include the names of other hoppers in humorous rhyme. This would cause much laughter among the travellers. One of the popular songs for the journey was:

> Sons of the sea,
> Bobbing up and down like this . . .

This was accompanied by actions, with all of the passengers in the crowded carriage on their feet bobbing up and down. It was amazing that the train managed to stay on the track. Other typical songs sung that were popular with the hoppers were Londoners' songs such as "Doing the Lambeth Walk" (rather difficult to act out in a crowded carriage) and, of course, "Maybe it's because I'm a Londoner".

The hop pickers were destined for several different stations along the railway which ran through the heart of Kent. As they left the train at their destinations they were met by a variety of conveyances, provided by the farmers, to take them to their respective farms. At the end of the season the hoppers would re-converge on the "Hoppers Special" for the return to their homes. For the majority of them this meant the East End of London, but for me it meant back to Essex.

When families arrived at their destination station, pandemonium broke out as they searched for their baggage which was in the luggage compartment at the rear of the train. Just when it seemed that the train would be unable to leave for the next station, miraculously, all parcels and trunks were restored to their rightful owner.

Our farmer would take us from the station in lorries or horse-drawn wagons to the common where the hop huts were situated. This was usually on high ground overlooking the lush green hop fields, which in a few weeks would be laid bare by the combined labour of the hop pickers. When arriving at our allocated hut the first task would be to unpack our belongings from the tea chests. These had been packed throughout the year as discarded clothes, toys and other unwanted items were added; at the time of unpacking many forgotten

13

treasures were uncovered. That previously discarded penknife with a broken blade became a very useful addition to my personal store.

The hop huts were made of corrugated iron which formed a long row of connected single rooms. Several such rows would be on one common. Each family was allocated a single room hut, about ten feet square. Sometimes as many as eight people would live in one hut. Often the rooms of related extended families were allocated adjacent to each other, if they were lucky! Some of the regular hoppers tried to make their huts more comfortable by white washing the corrugated iron walls, and by putting up curtains at the door (there were no windows).

The hop huts allowed little privacy within them or between them. All that separated one family's hut from the next was the ill-fitting corrugated wall. Consequently, all conversations and disputes could be clearly heard in many nearby huts. Flatulence drew much mirth to neighbours and embarrassment to the sufferer.

In the darkness of the late evening, disjointed, quiet-voiced conversations passed between the women from one darkened hut to another, "Do you remember, Mol, when your ol" man blew all his wages on that set of encyclopaedias?" "Yeh, silly sod. Pointless really. We've sold em now. He reckons he knows everything anyway, so why did he bother?" — "Lil, do you remember all the fuss your Bert made when he found out you'd pawned his fob watch?" "Nah, us married women should forget their mistakes, there's no point in two people remembering the same thing — men never forget!"

Another amusing conversation was taking place between Ada and Betty. Ada and her husband, Sid, were elderly and had occupied the same hut for years. Sid was a surly sod and too old for war service. Betty Knowles was a relatively young woman with two children, and it was her first season hop picking.

"Is Mr Knowles here?" Ada called across the croaking frogs of the night. "If he were he'd be a sensation," Betty replied. "He's been dead for four years." "Oh dear," Ada said, "What have I said, I'm sorry." "Don't be silly," Betty retorted, "I'm not bothered, so why should you be?"

"I sometimes wonder which is worse, divorce or death. After all, people do sometimes get back together after a divorce," Ada ruminated seriously. "It's difficult to get back together after death, thank God," Sid acidly commented.

"Well we were both," said Betty. "We divorced, and then he died. Neither was particularly upsetting for me!"

Nobody complained about these late night conversations, no matter how late. Eventually they subsided as the occupants of the huts fell asleep.

Each hut had about one third of its area allocated to a ready built wooden platform which served as a communal bed for all the family. Every family was allocated a bale of straw. This was spread on the platform to form bedding. The more enterprising hoppers took along large sacks like mattress covers ("ticks") which they stuffed with straw to form a kind of mattress.

We had a single acknowledgement of luxury in my grandmother's hut. This was a rag rug that adorned the rough concrete floor of the hut. It was multi-coloured with no set pattern. You could say it was abstract, but more likely "distract". My grandmother had made it out of bits of old clothes. It was backed with sacking that still smelt of the dried hops it once contained.

My first experience of hop picking was at the age of four when I accompanied my grandmother and my aunts, who, as mentioned earlier, were not a lot older than me. My mother was obliged to stay at home with my younger sister, and my father was engaged in war work. We went to a farm that we called "Clover Field". This initiation into hop picking took place in the years of the Second World War.

At first the novelty of sleeping five or six in a big bed was exciting. Later I was not so sure. The room was lit by a hurricane lamp which conjured up all kinds of frightening monsters on the walls. These were cleverly dispelled by my aunts who had the dexterity of creating friendly shadows such as rabbits and birds with their hands.

No sooner had I got over the terror of ogres on the walls than a new nightmare began; the orchestra of frogs croaking. My aunts' assurances were of little avail once a hysterical scream was heard from several huts away. This was followed by a plaintive wail, "Bloody hell, Dolly, there's a frog in my bed". Aunt Rita was quickly despatched by my grandmother to rescue the poor lady from a fate worse than death.

For the first few nights of sleeping the straw tended to be spiky because it was new. As a tot with a tender rear end, I was continually complaining, "There's straw sticking in my bum, Nan", much to the amusement of the occupants of the nearby huts. This was the signal for my aunts to bounce up and down on my part of the bed to break the straw down. Later our bedding became more comfortable with continual use, but towards the end of our stay it was more compact, hard and less restful, but always beautifully warm.

Cooking took two forms; on primus stoves or on open fires. High-tech families had a primus stove which could be used inside the huts. These always terrified the life out of me. They consisted of a brass chamber that was filled with paraffin oil. The chamber had a pump which was used to increase the pressure in it and cause the paraffin to be pushed out in a fine stream through a minute hole in a protruding stem. But the stem had to be hot in order for the paraffin to vaporise as it left the chamber. This was achieved initially by burning a lip full of methylated spirit around the stem until it was hot. Pumping the paraffin through the hot stem created a fine vapour that could be lit, achieving a fierce and roaring economical flame. But many people ended up with singed eyebrows and hair as a result of lighting the paraffin before the methylated spirit had done its job. Primus stoves were even operated by young children then. Most people today would be appalled by children being exposed to such a danger, especially in the confinement of rows of connected huts.

Most cooking took place on open fires outside the huts, when weather permitted. Each hut had its own open fire cooking arrangement, which merely consisted of an iron bar supported across a wood fire by a metal stand. There were also communal cooking areas between groups of huts. These were more substantially built, often with a tin roof affair to give some protection from the rain, but still largely open to the elements.

"'Opping pots" were essential hop pickers' equipment. These were heavy iron cauldrons that were positioned on the cooking pole by strong "S" shaped hooks. The fires were made from brush wood called "faggots". The latter were provided by the farmers in a communal pile some safe distance from the huts. It was the job of the children to ensure that a ready supply of faggots was kept by their hut.

The most common main meal fare for hoppers was stew which everyone, even children, could produce. Variations in taste were achieved by using different meats, e.g. bacon hocks, lamb, and corned beef. Local rabbits were a favourite, if one didn't question too deeply how they were obtained! Chicken was considered too expensive a meat to be used in stew. Mushrooms were abundant and free in the local fields, and the illicit raids on the farmer's onions and other vegetables were considered fair game and a source of cheap food. There was an abundance of wild herbs for those knowledgeable enough to recognise them.

The leftovers from one day's meal was left in the cauldron and added to the next day with further ingredients. From day to day meats and vegetables and herbs and spices would be added to vary the flavour. By the weekend the mixture had become a confusion of taste and the cauldron would be completely cleaned out to start a new week. A particular luxury I enjoyed was a jacket potato cooked to a cinder in the open fire, and the tasty inside scooped out. The art of eating a hoppers jacket potato was being able to eat the flesh, without getting any cinders in your mouth.

All water was obtained from standpipes situated at various places around the site. It was, usually, the task of children to collect the water in a variety of containers. By the time we got back to the hut with our buckets of water, our wellie boots were also awash inside. For me the standpipes were important meeting places with other children when we devised all kinds of devilment which invariably ended up with us soaking wet.

The communal toilets (often referred to as the "thunder box" — for obvious reasons!) were a crude and unsanitary arrangement set up at a discrete distance downwind from the huts. They consisted of small corrugated adjoined privies with a wide wooden plank and a hole positioned over a large tin drum, which was emptied periodically by the farmers. Male and female used the same toilets (can you imagine the cries that would come from the European Parliament today?), and the only concession to privacy was a bolt on the door. There were no windows and despite the considerable gaps in the doors and walls, the smell was overpowering in hot weather, and was only slightly alleviated by the crude disinfectant and other chemicals used. Perched on the wooden plank seat, with my feet dangling well above the floor, I was always terrified that I would fall through the hole and into the smelly drum below. Bum balancing became a fine art!

Each morning the hoppers awoke early. First there was the procession of chamber pots and overnight buckets to the toilet for emptying. These were followed by visits for "sit downs". The majority of those going to the toilets clutched roughly torn squares of newspaper. The more well-to-do marched down the hill proudly displaying toilet rolls.

The less hardy people would wash inside the huts, perhaps with the luxury of a bowl of warm water. The more seasoned campaigner washed out in the open with cold water. This was followed by a quick and basic breakfast. Next was the important task of preparing sandwiches and drinks for the day. These were essential to keep us going while we were working in the hopfields. The standard drink was orange squash made from National Health Service supplements for children.

A typical hop picking morning started early with a cold damp sunrise, and the morning mist still hovering. Spiders' webs hung heavy with dew, and the smell of the fires outside the huts hung in the air. A nippy breeze assured you that the winter frosts were not far away. By eight o'clock in the morning everyone had to be assembled in the hop fields, but there were rarely latecomers because this was why the hoppers had really come — to earn a meagre supplement to their normal income. A hard-working adult could earn about £12 during the four week's picking.

On the first day of picking there was an early morning "briefing", when the families were allocated the bins into which they would pick the hops. At this time we would also be told the rules the farmer wanted followed, e.g. no raiding the fruit orchards, and the "tally", which is the payment per bushel of hops picked, e.g. four bushels to the shilling. Sometimes the tally became a subject of heated argument between the pickers and the grower when it was considered that the tally was not fair. At this time the pickers would also be warned about picking "dirty" hops. This referred to having too many leaves in the bin.

The hop "bines" grow from a crown sending up tendril-like growths. Each hop plant had four harsh sisal strings spreading out vertically like a square cone, with the widest spacing at the top. These stretched up to a combination of upright and diagonal poles set in rows, and criss-crossed with a network of overhead wires. The bottom three feet of strings were constrained by a horizontal string called the "cradle". Four tendrils of hop bines were trained up each string, resulting in sixteen stems from one mature hop plant. When I first went hop picking, much of the preparation of the supports for the growing hops was carried out by farm workers on stilts. Who needed to go to a circus when there were so many versatile farm workers around us?

Hop bines carry rich clusters of green cone-like flowers, rather like grapes on a vine. They form a forest-like growth of lush green, towering to a height of twelve feet. The bines have coarse, hairy branches that scratch wherever they touch the skin. The bines stretch in long straight lines, or "alleys", the length of the hop field, forming a seemingly impenetrable jungle. At the start of the picking each hop row looked like a long green tunnel of leaves with the pungent smelling hops glistening with the morning dew or overnight rain.

The hops were picked into a large "bin", although on some farms they were picked straight into bushel baskets. The bin was about seven feet long and consisted of two ends made of crossed pieces of strong wood, and joined by two sturdy wooden side rails, extended at the ends to form "handles" which were used for moving the bin. The side rails supported a long sacking bag to form a kind of trough some three feet wide. These trestles were strong and stable enough to support four adults sat on each corner whilst they picked the hops into the bin. They were light enough to be moved along the rows of hops by two people, but to move it when fully loaded with hops required the combined strength of four adults. One bin would be used by an entire family.

The hop pickers moved along the maze of rows, pulling on the coarse bines until the string broke, allowing the coarse hairy bines to fall, showering the hoppers with water from the overnight rain and dew, pollen, and all kinds of insects. Several bines would be pulled down to be draped across the hop bin. All who were old enough were expected to pick the silky, sticky, green-yellow hops. Children not tall enough to reach the bin side rails would be given a box or an upturned umbrella to put their picked hops into.

Sometimes a bine, or the string supporting it, would stubbornly refuse to break. This was the signal for as many children as possible to swing on the vine together until the string broke, dumping the kids in an untidy heap of giggling bodies on the ground. When a bine still refused to come down a worker, called a "pole puller", was summoned. He would use a long pole with a sharp hook on the end to cut the offending overhead string.

The hop picking family would work along between the rows of bines, picking off the flower heads, and trying to avoid getting too many leaves in the bin. During the picking the thumb and forefinger became blackened by the pale green flowers. This was caused by the pollen or by the chemicals the farmers sprayed on the hops. This blackening tasted bitter, in a way similar to the taste of the residue left from picking tomatoes.

There were no toilets out in the hop fields. The procedure for "going" was to walk some way ahead of the pickers and squat in the rich leafy lanes ahead where there was some privacy. The problem was that in due course the pickers would eventually arrive at the same spot as they progressed along the alley. Then it was a case of "tread carefully".

Children old enough to do so picked alongside their mothers, whilst younger ones might be lucky enough to be given the glorious freedom of wandering among the bines playing hide and seek. For me the greatest pleasure was to wander alone among the quiet leafy green aisles. It seemed like a fairyland where one was cut off from civilisation. The ringing of a bell was sure to bring all the children to their mother's side. The bell announced the arrival of the lollipop man. If the day's work had been pretty successful then you might be rewarded with a lollipop, a mint humbug, sherbet dabs or aniseed balls.

During the war years I was fortunate to be considered too young to pick hops alongside the adults, so I was left very much to my own devices. Whilst the young girls tended to search for pretty pieces of broken glass and china, the boys would explore the local countryside. I spent many happy hours wandering in the local woods, where the fruits of nature, such as nuts, apples and blackberries, sustained me throughout my travels. There were also treasures to be collected and taken back to show the adults. My favourite trophies were spent shells and shot off pieces of the aircraft that could be seen engaged in battles high above the fields of Kent. The pickers carried on picking even during air raids.

As enemy aircraft flew overhead, we could see the puffs of smoke that surrounded them as they flew through the anti-aircraft fire. After such an event the fields were frequently littered with shrapnel and all sorts of evidence of the attack, which were exciting prizes for children to find. Apart from spent shells and bits shot off aircraft, one of my most exciting finds was a substantial chunk off a magnetic mine.

The hop-fields were situated in what later became known as "Doodlebug Alley"; the flight path of the rockets aimed at London. On one occasion, during the later years of the war, there was all the usual banter going on between the pickers, then suddenly they all went silent and the ominous sound of a doodlebug penetrated the silence. Everyone waited for the fatal time when the engine of the rocket would stop, signalling the ultimate disaster for some poor soul. Then a young girl from London began screaming uncontrollably from the memory of horror the sound brought back to her. The incident also served to remind me of my own recent experience of a doodlebug.

After the war I went hop picking with my parents and my brother and sister. My father would work at the Ford Motor Company in Dagenham during the week, and then he would come to see us at weekends, often cycling all the way from Essex to the hop farm to save on the train fare. We were not wealthy enough to buy one of the cars he worked all week producing.

During one winter we had to abandon a planned visit to our hop hut to prepare it for the next season. It was January of 1947, which was the worst winter on record at that time. Even the River Thames froze that year. Just walking from our back door to the street was an enormous task for my little seven year old legs, so deep was the snow. It was impossible to see where the side of the road ended, and even more importantly where the dykes by the side of the road were.

During the picking season on the farms, lunchtime would usually be spent in the fields sitting on a pile of stripped bines, munching on sandwiches, and trying to avoid too much of the bitter-tasting hop blackening getting into your mouth. But, no matter what the filling of the sandwiches was, the bitter taste of the hop pollen disguised it completely. A few people would wear rubber gloves while picking, but these were the exception as most people agreed that wearing gloves slowed down the amount you were able to pick.

Tea would be available to those fortunate enough to own a thermos flask. Often pickers would mix up tea containing milk and sugar in a "billy can". This would then be heated up on an open fire in the field. We didn't have a flask for tea, and sometimes it wasn't convenient to light a fire in the fields, for example, when it was raining. One of the answers was to make tea in the morning and put it in a stone hot water bottle, and then wrap it in a towel to keep it warm until tea break time.

Sometimes a "well-to-do" hop picker was fortunate enough to have a portable radio to play in the fields, and all could hear the familiar sound of *Workers Playtime*, introduced by the classic theme music of Eric Coates, "Call your workers".

During the day, farm workers would go behind the pickers and cut off the stripped bines near the base. These would be carried away by wagons drawn by huge shire horses or tractors. Children moved around the horses seemingly oblivious to any danger. However, I was always timid when near them and this fear has remained with me through to adulthood. The final view of the picked and cleared field looked like an area that had been attacked by locusts.

Late in the afternoon a crew of farm workers, called "tally-men", would come round to measure the pickings of each family. This was a time of abuse and ribald comments. The hops were measured using a bushel basket. The "tally" for a bushel of hops was set at the start of the season, and the rules were that hops should be picked free from leaves, although this was impossible to achieve and a compromise quality was the realistic aim. The bushel basket was scooped into the bin and each full one was tipped into large sacks called "pokes", thus measuring the picker's output and income.

Before the tally-men arrived the pickers would try to fluff up their hops so that they would take up as much room as possible in the basket. When a tally-man was considered too heavy handed in pushing his basket into the hops he would be cursed by the hoppers for deliberately crushing the flowers and reducing the overall quantity. The tally-man would often be told to do something impossible to himself! It was uncomfortable to pick hops when it was raining, but when they were wet they made a bigger quantity in the measuring baskets because they were so swollen by the dampness. To some extent, this compensated for getting wet while picking.

The process of scooping out the flowers was overseen by the team foreman, or even the farm owner himself. He would count the bushels of hops and record the tally for each bin, adding it to the previous total. Sometimes the foreman would refuse to allow a bin to be emptied because it contained too many leaves. The family would then be left to clean out as many leaves as possible before the tally-men finished their rounds. To be told that their hops contained too many leaves offended the pride of the hoppers.

In the early days of my hop picking experience, horse drawn carts were used to transport the large sacks (called "pokes") containing the hops to the kilns. Later the horses were replaced by tractors. At the kilns the hops were dried by charcoal or oil fired heating. We children were not allowed into the kiln areas, but I was once given the chance to see what went on there. However, I found the heat and the smell too overpowering to ever want to visit again.

One of the things I hated about hop picking was the great big caterpillars which looped over the bines and dropped on us. One clever Dick said that they belonged to the hawk moth. This knowledge did not reduce my revulsion of these creatures.

When children had picked what was considered their quota of hops as a contribution to the family's collection, usually by lunch time, they were allowed to go off and amuse themselves. This was a time when the hop garden resounded with the sound of children at play and engaging in adventures that only children can conjure up. This was a time when the mothers would gossip to neighbours and friends picking nearby.

The picking days were very long. Although we had to be on the field by eight o'clock, we were often on there as early as seven in the morning, and rarely stopped work until the whistle blew at four in the afternoon. The call would then come to "Pick no more bines" and the day's picking was over. Children were called back;

coats and other things were gathered for the tramp back to the common, the huts, and the evening meal.

In the evening there was a lot of good-natured banter and singing around the fires. Sometimes there would be someone who could play the accordion or a mouth organ, and this was sure to get the singing going. But, to be honest, it didn't take much to get the friendly hoppers joking and singing.

A visit to the local shop always interested me, not only because of the wide range of things sold, but I was also fascinated by the wire mesh in front of the shop counters. At home I only saw this wire mesh in the local Post Office, but here all of the shops seemed to have it. It was not until many years later I found out the reason for this. Normally, prior to the hopping season, merchandise would be stacked outside on the pavement in fine weather, and many items hung for close inspection around the shop to tempt shoppers. However, once the hoppers arrived in the area all goods were protected behind the counters and wire mesh partitions. Hoppers were not to be tempted — or trusted!

Being sent to the shops was for me an occasion for adventure. We always chose the most torturous of routes. Scrambling along a narrow alley behind a barn, wading through a running stream, hurtling across the field where the supposedly "wild" bull roamed. We followed any route other than the easy way, by road.

We would arrive at the shop dirty and dishevelled, in holey jumpers and trousers, and wearing our ever present wellie boots. It was hardly surprising that the shopkeepers treated us with disdain and suspicion. One day I returned from a shopping expedition with one of my aunts bearing a crusty loaf. Our hunger got the better of us on the return journey and we had picked out the inside of the loaf, leaving a crusty shell. We were incredulous that no one would believe us when we said, "The mice must have got at it."

I loved the camaraderie that abounded among hop pickers, and this was particularly apparent at night time. In the evenings the common area of the huts site glowed with the many fires outside the huts and, if the weather was reasonable, all the families would sit around the fires on homemade stools chatting. This was a time when children were allowed to experiment in cooking toast, baked potatoes, and apples pinched from the local orchards. A special evening treat was a mug of dry baby milk powder mixed with cocoa and sugar and eaten dry, again, courtesy of the National Health Service.

Scrumping was considered a normal extension of hop picking and, try as he might, the farmer couldn't possibly prevent it. When I was about ten years old and working on a hop farm in Kent, I initiated my younger brother and sister into the noble art of scrumping. One day when we were returning from a scrumping expedition, we were challenged by the farmer. "Have you been scrumping in my orchard?" he demanded. Our denial was promptly followed by a cascade of fruit bursting out from the bottom of my trousers; the contraband had been hidden in my trouser legs which had not been, as I thought, firmly tucked into my wellie boots! We took flight and spent the rest of the day worrying that the farmer would turn up on the common and send our family home in disgrace. But it didn't happen.

The real experts at scrumping were the gypsies who frequented many hop farms. They extended their haul of illicit food to chickens, eggs and rabbits, or so I was told by the adults. They were regarded with suspicion by hoppers and farmers alike, but they were hard workers. They would continue to pick in all weathers, even heavy rain. For this reason their work was held in high regard by the farmers. The other pickers would also work during the rain, but tended to do so with less enthusiasm than the gypsies.

The gypsies usually occupied a section of the common separate from the other hoppers. Often they would make up an area with their own caravans rather than use the huts that were available. Although many of the hoppers were wary of them, I got on well with them.

Romany families were present on most hop farms. Many would meet and stay for the whole of the season, which was longer than just the hop picking period, and continued into fruit picking. They always seemed a proud race to me and did not appear to mix readily with the rest of us pickers. Some people were hostile towards them but I found them both mysterious and interesting, and I spent a lot of time safely in their company. They taught me how to find the appropriate leaves which could be rubbed on my legs to instantly dispel the discomfort caused by stinging nettles, which

31

grew in abundance around the hop fields. Their life was far from easy and they always seemed to work with a greater intensity than the rest of us. But whatever hardships their way of life entailed, it always seemed to me that they were compensated with a greater degree of freedom.

The gypsies had many words that were special to them. They used to call me "chavvie" (child) and their teenage children "chie" (young woman) and "rai" (young man). My family were referred to as "gorgio" or "gorgie" (non-gypsy) and the gypsy home as "vardo" (caravan). They told me what seemed wonderful tales of their life on the "drom" (road). It all seemed exciting to me and was further enhanced by their strange words. But I also learned of their aversion to the word "diddecoi", which was used by many of the hoppers to refer to gypsies. I learnt that this was really a derogatory term for gypsy implying a half-breed.

You either loved hop picking or you hated it. In the morning it was generally cold, and you got wet with the dew as the bines were pulled. In the afternoon it tended to get hot, so you often got burnt by the sun. When you got back to the hut you were tired and dirty, and there was no bath to soak in and freshen up. A strip wash, hopefully in warm water, was the best to hope for.

The weekends were important times because this was when many husbands and fathers would come to visit, especially during the war years when those engaged in reserved occupations would come to see their family. Picking, if it took place at all, finished early on Saturday. This was a time to visit local shops and go to the Saturday matinee at the local cinema. In the evenings there would be a walk to the local pub, where we children sat outside with our lemonade and a bag of crisps.

On one such weekend during wartime, I was with my grandmother amongst a group of hoppers that were sitting near a bridge over a river at the bottom of a hill, and near the river some German prisoners of war were working in the fields. An open-backed lorry, carrying women and children hoppers, ran out of control on the hill and crashed into the river. The German prisoners jumped into the water to save the people and emerged to the cheers of the onlookers. I remember thinking at that time that these terrible men we were continually being warned about could not be so bad, and in this instance the "enemy" became the hero!

Sometimes a mobile cinema would visit the common and show a film in the open air. This would be considered a big occasion, especially if we managed to get through a whole film without getting drenched by rain. Everyone took their wooden stools, which, as previously mentioned, were often homemade, and "doorstep" sandwiches to munch during the show.

One Sunday morning during the war, we emerged from the hop huts to find a large trader's van abandoned on the top of the hill of the common. It had been "borrowed" from the local village by some of the older teenagers to get back from the pub. The unlocked van was too much of a temptation for us young children. We clambered all over it, taking turns in "driving" it on imaginary journeys through war-torn

Europe. Soon parents were recognising a possible danger and calling their children away, and I found myself in the joyous position of sole driver. Then I heard my grandmother, who was not one to be disobeyed, roar out my name. No sooner had I jumped clear of the van than it charged down the hill, through the faggot pile, and into the lake at the bottom of the hill. I was conspicuous by my absence when the police called later to investigate.

Sunday afternoon was weapon production time for young people. We made bows and arrows, spears and catapults from material that was abundantly available in the local woods, and string abandoned in the hop fields once the bines had been pulled. Much time was given to elaborately carving the weapons by removing the green bark to leave intricate patterns in the white flesh below the soft bark. My treasured broken pen knife came into its own on these afternoons.

I don't remember the weapons ever being used in an offensive way, or even for hunting. They were mainly for a show of workmanship of carving, although occasionally they would be used to demonstrate marksmanship. Dangerous though it seems today, even with hoards of kids armed with bows and arrows and homemade spears and daggers, I cannot recall a single injury, although parents were forever reminding us of the fate of King Harold in the Battle of Hastings, which took place not far away from the hop farm.

For a few years we changed from the farm where we had usually worked to another one in Sevenoaks in Kent. A short, intricate walk away from the hop fields ran a railway line. This carried the express trains that ran down to the south coast to link London with the Channel ferries. The railway line was out of bounds to children for safety reasons. A group of us went there as often as possible. One of the older members of our "gang" used to place a penny on the railway line to see what the train would do to it. I never carried out this dangerous experiment, only because pennies were far too valuable to me!

Across the other side of the railway line ran a small, shallow river, from which we would catch tiny fish to feed to the wild cats that roamed the hop picking area. Yet further on, across two cow fields, there was a small dense orchard. It had certainly been planned and cultivated in some distant past, but had been abandoned for a long time for some reason. The now distorted branches of the trees still held an abundance of fruit, particularly plums, apples and pears. I once picked a single apple there that weighed almost a pound. The fruit was freely available, but the fun of plundering did not match the thrill of scrumping from the cultivated forbidden orchards belonging to the hop farms.

In the dark centre of the wild orchard, lay hidden a small abandoned cottage. This was clearly the home of the original owners of the orchard, and now it lay in decay. To us kids it became the "haunted cottage", in which, of course, lived an unseen wicked witch! So vivid had this description become that we never crossed the boundary of its broken picket fence.

35

One day I decided I would climb over the fence into the rambling garden, notwithstanding a "Trespassers Will Be Prosecuted" notice. I scaled the fence, with some scraping of my already scarred knees, and jumped down into the unkempt grass the other side. I got to my feet and looked anxiously around. The thick trunks of ancient trees initially hid the house from my view. But eventually I found myself on an overgrown path that wound through the trees. On both sides the grass grew high and it was easy to imagine that no one had been there for a very long time. I breasted the tall grass and my feet took me to the veranda that ran along one side of the house. Just as I made to step up onto the veranda in order to look through the window, there was a shrill screech and something flew past my head just touching me. This was the signal for me to take flight and I left the area far faster than I had arrived. Needless to say, when I later bragged of my brave deeds to my friends, none of them believed I had been brave enough to approach the "witch's lair".

Part of the fun of going hop picking was that there was little fuss over our appearance, or continual demands to keep clean. But it had its funny side. Coming back to the huts one evening with my friend from the hut next door, he said to his mum, "Who am I?" His mum, willing to play the game, said, "I don't know! Who are you?" "Wow", he cried, "Mrs Miles was right! She said I was so dirty, my own mother wouldn't recognise me!"

At the end of the hop picking season the hop pickers were "paid off" by the farmer prior to leaving the hop farm to return home. The money they were paid would be the sum of the tally recorded against the name of the family during the weeks of picking. However, there was also a tradition of "subbing". This involved the grower paying the picker a proportion of their wages to tide them over until the picking was completed. For some families this meant that at the end of the picking season they might have very little to show for the labour, other than Wellington boot marks around their calves. But for most of the hoppers the main benefit was that they had had some form of a holiday.

Often the pickers would immediately book their next season with the farmer before they even left the farm, thus ensuring "their" hut was retained for them. But sometimes they would decide that it was time for a change and they would book for the next season with a farm in a different area of Kent.

In spite of the restrictions on supplies during the war years, I don't remember ever being hungry. Perhaps it was because I didn't need to eat much, especially with all the illicit treats that could be obtained at nature's (or the farmer's) expense. But it may have been because my family saw it as important that youngsters were fed adequately. Even after the war there were still shortages, and in fact it wouldn't be until the early 1950s that rationing would end in Britain. The 1950s were the years of my early teens, and then it seemed that I was always hungry — one of the effects of the onset of adolescence!

Needless to say by the time the hop picking season was over, we children had missed some four or even five weeks of school. For this reason we were of course unhappy to have to return home. The school was not particularly happy either! A couple of weeks before the half term break there would be an influx of ex-London families that had been hop-picking. In a single school on Canvey Island at least a dozen of these children were from our family alone, and there were many other families in the school who also went hopping.

Hop picking children were sometimes taunted by other children who had learnt from their parents to look down on hop picking, and we often denied that this was where we had been. However, our rosy cheeks, sunburnt hands and face, and the tell tale dark wellie boot line worn around our calves gave the game away.

The taunts directed at us hop picking kids were hurtful, but also confusing for me. The implication seemed to be that only poor children went hop picking, but most of the other kids were no better off than we were. In fact, few of the other kids had any sort of a holiday at all. But, in spite of the taunts and the stigma attached to it, I knew at the time that I enjoyed the experience immensely.

I have been on holidays to many exotic places in far flung places of the world since those formative days of my life. It doesn't matter where I have gone, nowhere has had the lasting influence of those years of hop picking in the fields of Kent, the Garden of England. I shall always be grateful that my parents and my grandparents gave me the opportunity to experience what is now a part of English history.

One year the education authority (Essex County Council) took my father to court for keeping us away from school. My father did not deny the charge but argued that it was the only way he could afford to give his family a holiday. The judge sympathised and fined him a token 5s. A couple of years after this we abandoned the tradition of the early years of my life.

Eventually, hop picking in the traditional manual way I had known for so much of my childhood began to die out. There were two main reasons for this. First, as the lot of the working class people began to improve in the post-war years, the need for working "holidays" became less necessary. Second, the development of machines to carry out hop picking made the need for manual labour less necessary. Add to these reasons the development of beers that contained no hops, and this led to the days of traditional hop picking being numbered.

Later, in adult life, I was the manager of the head office of a large company and part of my job was to organise the holiday rota. I asked one young secretary where she was going on her holiday. She answered with some embarrassment, "I'm going somewhere that you wouldn't consider very proper, but if you must know, I'm going hop picking with my parents". Little did she realise that hop picking had played such an important part of my young life.

CHAPTER
TWO

FLOODS OF TEARS

By no stretch of imagination can Canvey Island be said to be a place of beauty, but I loved the island during my school years. I loved the disorderly way that the streets were laid out, with little apparent forward planning; they were of varying widths, and often little more than gravel tracks. And there was the network of ditches and dykes that not only provided essential drainage for a place entirely below sea level, but also gave so much fun and adventure for young limbs.

What I recognised, even at a very young age, was the community spirit that prevailed. I loved knowing I was part of a world that valued care for others, and demonstrated this openly. People from the mainland often referred to the "Islanders" in a disparaging way, but soon learnt to expect the sting of a well-aimed response to unguarded remarks. The people of Canvey obeyed the old adage, "I may criticise my own, but just beware if you try to!"

But it was a limiting place in some ways. During my early years, I felt confined by the community. So many youngsters, it seemed, left school and took employment in small factories and local shops, never venturing far from the island. I worried that I might remain trapped within the close, and largely closed, community. I had imagination and curiosity, and I wanted to learn and see more about the wider world. To remain on Canvey seemed too easy to me. It would hold me back; prevent me from testing myself, making my own way in the world.

Later, but still in my teens, I was to have the experience of travelling the world. In all my travels I saw many places of great beauty and wonder that confirmed I was right to seek to escape the confines of the island, but I never lost the urge to return to the bosom of the island community. Probably one of the best examples of community spirit was reflected in the local fire brigade.

In the early 1950s the population of Canvey Island was just over 11,000. The community was a close and intimate one. Most of the inhabitants were familiar with prominent members of the community and those providing essential services.

The local fire brigade members were endeared to the residents of Canvey, not only for the emergency service they provided, but also by their often humorous antics. Several members of my family were voluntary firemen and a few of the firemen, including my father, were members of the local council. An example of the humour of the firefighters is reflected in a leaflet that they had printed for distribution at a charity fundraising event, which aimed to raise money to build a community hall that would commemorate those who had died during the war.

The leaflet asked residents to complete a questionnaire and post it to the fire brigade if their services were required. The leaflet asked questions such as:

Address of fire?
Is it near a pub?
If we come, will you help us?
Are you on the sewer?
How many lavatories do you have?
Would your children interfere with our hoses?
Would you have a cup of tea ready for us?
Should we take 2 days to get there, would you keep it going until we arrive?

They even, humorously, included a "price list" for their services. Calls by pubs and tobacconists were free. Private fires were charged at 7s 6d, of which 2s 6d was given to the person who gave the alarm call.

The fire brigade was a volunteer force, and was overseen by a single full-time officer named Griffiths, usually referred to as "Griff". Griff took his responsibilities seriously and he tried to keep his squad as focused as possible on their responsibilities, but he had his hands full as their sense of fun and team spirit overrode any form of "officialdom". The members of the fire brigade were paid a nominal monthly retainer fee and a set payment for each call out.

The firemen were summoned to the fire station by the sounding of the old wartime air raid siren, which blasted clear across the whole of the island. The siren was later to be supplemented by electric alarms in the home of each fireman. At the piercing wail of the siren the volunteers would race from their home, or place of work, to the fire station by whatever transport they could commandeer — usually the nearest bicycle. One of the firemen was employed as a milkman and another in bakery deliveries; both involved the use of hand carts. Following the call of the siren, a milk float or bakery barrow could be seen abandoned by the side of the road until the fireman returned to collect it. Nothing was stolen from these abandoned carts in those times as their owners raced to the aid of the community. And customers never complained about delayed deliveries.

The first fireman to arrive at the station, who was qualified to drive the ancient fire engine, would move it out of the station to the forecourt and wait until sufficient volunteers had arrived to man the machine before racing off to the scene of the fire. At this time of coal burning fires, chimney fires were common. There were also many small farms on the island, so grass fires would frequently occur during a hot summer. Some of the grass fires were caused by natural combustion, some by sheer carelessness, such as a cigarette butt or a discarded bottle, and a few were deliberately started by wayward youngsters.

If we kids happened to be near the fire station when the alarm sounded, some of us would race after the fire engine on our bikes as it careered through the streets on the way to the fire. We could never keep up with it of course, but on such a small island, it was rarely difficult to find where the fire was. This enabled us to watch our local heroes at work and injected some excitement into our days.

The fire engine was an old-fashioned but glamorous machine with lots of brass and a hand-rung bell. There was only limited space in the driving cab and so the engine raced through the narrow streets, many of which were unmade, with firemen clinging to the standing places on the rear of the machine in various stages of dress as they struggled into their fire-fighting gear, much to the amusement of residents as they watched them speed past. Some firemen who had not arrived in time to clamber aboard the fire engine would follow to the scene of the fire on their bicycles.

The procedure of the local police station at the time of a fire was that a police officer would be sent to any fire, post-haste, by bicycle. It was often the case that the fire engine would pass the police officer peddling furiously along their route. On one cold, windy and rainy occasion, the driver of the fire engine took pity on the police officer and stopped to give him a lift to the fire. Good sense? After all they were going to the same fire! The good deed was rewarded by the policemen reporting the driver for speeding. Needless to say, no police officer was picked up after this incident. One fireman was heard to mutter after this incident that he would pay his kid to set fire to the policeman's shed at the bottom of his garden, and then refuse to turn out to put the fire out.

A source of amusement, for us youngsters, arose when the fire engine was being closely followed to a blaze by a police car. The engine driver took a turn into a wrong "no through" road. The fireman driver threw the fire engine into reverse and, you guessed it! The fire engine was not badly damaged but, needless to say, the police car was a mess.

On another occasion, whilst fighting a difficult blaze at the local wood yard, the crew took the engine within the wood yard with the intention of fighting the fire from the inside and closer to the blaze. There was a change in wind direction that caused the flames to create a horseshoe shape, and the fire engine was in danger of becoming trapped in a ring of fire. The team bravely rescued their vehicle by driving it through a gap in the searing heat of the flames to safety. But their bravery was rewarded by a fine and a reprimand from fire headquarters for leaving one of their hoses behind to be destroyed in the fire.

One of the difficulties Canvey faced in those days was that if two fires occurred at once, the single fire engine could not be in two places at the same time. In such circumstances a fire station on the mainland would be notified to send an engine to fill in the gap. This obviously resulted in delays in arrival of the fire crew to the second fire call. One such event was to reveal a local hero.

One Sunday, while the Canvey fire crew were attending an extensive grass fire on a farm, a second fire was reported at an unattended builder's yard in a heavily populated area of the island. This was endangering other nearby buildings, and a call was made summoning a backup fire tender from the mainland.

During the delay of arrival of the mainland fire crew, neighbours of the builder's yard stood helplessly outside the locked gates of the yard. Then, suddenly, a known local scallywag, Dave, came racing round the corner in his tatty old jeep. Without slowing down the slightest, he smashed through the gates into the centre of the yard. He jumped out and, to everyone's astonishment, started to smother the flames with heavy canvas sheets he tore off of the builder's stock. Soon the neighbours gathered their wits and joined him in the fight.

When the fire crew and the builder eventually arrived at the scene, the fire was already extinguished. The local press and a couple of councillors arrived, and Dave was declared the hero of the moment. The newspaper reporter summed it up by saying that Dave's prompt response was one of the most courageous acts he had seen for some time.

The builder was so grateful to Dave that he rewarded him with £50 (as much as he had paid for his old jeep). The newspaper reporter asked Dave, "What are you going to do with the money?" He thought for a minute and then said, "Well, for a start, I think I should get the brakes fixed on that bloody jeep before it kills me."

The fire team were regular and popular participants in the local carnival, which raised money for local charities. This consisted of a long line of decorated floats on the open backs of lorries, each depicting scenes for the interest and amusement of crowds, who came from far and wide to line the route which wound throughout the main roads of Canvey. The aim of the annual carnival was to raise funds for local charities. An important recipient of the proceeds collected was the previously mentioned local community hall that was built as a memorial to commemorate those from the community who had lost their lives during the war.

At one carnival the firemen had the crowds in stitches with the antics of a laundry, with many onlookers becoming sprayed with water and suds. At another carnival they became a mobile bakery and many people left the route with a heavy dusting of flour. The firemens' carnival float was always the centre of attraction and a great money raiser.

The final curtain on the firemen's carnival participation occurred when a fire call came whilst they were trapped in the long queue of carnival floats a considerable way from the fire station, causing a delay in their attendance at the blaze. Shortly following this incident the fire crew were directed that they could no longer participate in activities which would delay their response to emergency calls. This timely reminder to the firemen to the importance of their emergency duties came at an opportune time, because they were soon to face the most severe test in their history.

It was the Dutch, with their special knowledge of drainage developed to protect their own low-lying country, who first successfully reclaimed Canvey Island from the sea in the seventeenth century. They did so with a sea wall surrounding the whole island, and a network of dykes to drain the 4,000 acres and, as it happened, in time to provide a harvest of wildlife for local children to investigate.

The island's walls, completed by the Dutch in 1623, were breached many times, including 1731, 1735, 1790, 1881 and 1897. Each time this happened they were strengthened and substantially reinforced and raised. This enabled them to withstand the worst of nature's onslaughts for many years, with only relatively minor flooding occurring. That was until the night of 31 January 1953.

The weather on this fateful night was foul with a gale developing in fury. But this was not unusual for coastal areas and, although some had heard the radio warning of possible flooding, this had been heard many times before and most people went innocently to bed. But the full extent of the danger was not conveyed to the population, because it was not fully recognised.

Nobody realised that the developing gale was coinciding with spring tides, forming a deadly cocktail that was to devastate Britain's coastline. The fury of nature grew in intensity as the gale turned to hurricane force and built a surge of water. The North Sea was eight feet above normal and began to batter the coastline.

The fire brigade served a relatively small urban community of 11,000 or so people. The housing on the island consisted mainly of flimsy bungalows and many of the roads were little more than dirt tracks. Many of the bungalows had at one time been holiday homes for the weekend use of London families. Since the war most of the holiday homes had been taken over to full-time residence, but the relatively flimsy structure of many of the homes remained.

Few families had television or central heating to keep people from their beds, and even telephones were rarely found in homes. And so, with the wind howling in fury outside, like most families that night we were happy to go to bed. It was the cosiest place to be. But some residents had attended a festival in the War Memorial Hall that had been opened for the first time that day. Little did those that attended this event realise, while returning home late that night, the drama that was about to unfold.

Because of my father's position as a member of the volunteer fire brigade, and a member of the local council, we had a recently installed alarm bell in our house to summon him to the fire station. We were also fortunate to have a telephone, not that common on Canvey at that time.

We first learnt of the impending disaster by a telephone call in the early hours of the morning as the flood occurred. The telephone switchboard operator telephoned my father to tell him that the sea wall had been badly breached. Shortly after this telephone call my father was summoned to the fire station, leaving myself, my mother and younger sister and brother at home alone.

My father went to help in the more severely hit parts of the island and my mother went round to warn our neighbours, many of whom did not fully comprehend the extent of the danger we were in because our part of the island initially showed little evidence of the problems that lay ahead. The response of many neighbours was, "Thanks, but we'll go back to our beds and see what it's like in the morning." This seemingly flippant response was not entirely unexpected, because the wall had been penetrated many times in the past, without serious consequences. By daylight the situation was obviously more serious than they had expected, and it was now too late for many people to do much to save their possessions. And for some it resulted in loss of life.

While my mother was warning neighbours, I prepared to abandon our house with my younger brother and sister. By this time there was no electricity and it was still dark, and our bungalow was surrounded by water. When my mother returned we decided to make our way to the local school, which was above water at that time. We were all distressed to see our cat perched on top of the shed at the bottom of the garden, but it was not possible to get to him, even though a neighbour made an attempt to rescue him, and was bitten for his efforts.

The flood water was rising around our home but it was still possible to walk to safety with the aid of Wellington boots, although too deep for my younger sister and brother. My mother carried my sister and I carried my brother. Before we left the house my mother told me to put some shoes in my pocket to change into later. When we eventually reached the school I felt quite heroic — I had carried my brother to safety. But my youthful ego was soon deflated when my mother berated me because I had put into my pockets one brown shoe and one black! End of dreams of heroic recognition.

The scene in the old school hall was dismal and brought back memories of wartime bombing disasters and nights in air raid shelters. Families sat around in a dishevelled state and wearing a strange assortment of hastily grabbed clothes. People were brought in by rescuers who had snatched them from rooftops into small rowing boats. Some of those rescued were injured through having to break their way through to the roof top where they were found. Others sustained injuries as they clambered from the roof into the boats.

At one time the lights in the hall were turned off to protect the modesty of an injured woman brought into the hall and wearing only the flimsiest of clothing. Those who had been on the roof of their home had been there for many hours, in mid-winter, and during a fierce gale that continued to blow throughout the night. As each newcomer came into the school hall they faced a sea of faces; most of the owners of these faces were looking for a sign of members of their family.

The drama of the situation we were in was reflected by an old lady in the description of her escape. Late at night, as she was preparing for bed, she went to pass through her sitting room, which was some four inches lower than other rooms. As she stepped into this room she found she was up to her ankles in ice-cold water. She could see the water bubbling up through the floorboards, and visibly rising. She hurried to her bedroom and clambered on to the bed. Before long the water was up to her waist. She clambered onto higher furniture until her head was touching the ceiling, and still the water rose. Then the electricity cut out and she was left in darkness, terrified that she would fall from her high, stooping refuge.

This elderly lady remained in this precarious position, scantily dressed and freezing cold for fifteen hours, until she was rescued by a man who had commandeered a small boat and was searching for survivors. She was taken to the school where so many of us were gathered awaiting transport to the mainland.

Eventually we were ferried off the island by a fleet of vehicles. Most of the single main road that existed at that time was fortunately still above water level at the exit end of the island. From the upper deck of the bus that ferried us to the mainland it was like travelling along a pier stretching out between the flooded fields. It was heartbreaking to see animals floating dead or marooned and jostling for safety on hillocks already overcrowded.

As we made our way off the island we passed our local pub, The Red Cow, to see a quite amazing sight. The pub stood on ground that was slightly higher than the surrounding area and the waters had not invaded it, whilst all the surrounding area was awash. For this reason, the pub became a command base for some of the rescue operations, much to the amusement of some of the force that arrived to snatch the island back from the sea. Some time later this pub was renamed The King Canute in recognition of the fact that it had withstood the onslaught of the sea, although it had not had the effect of actually turning the tide!

As the bus made its way towards the only bridge allowing access to the mainland, we could see from our position high on the top deck, broken tree limbs trapped against the walls of houses, and furniture floating in a bobbing motion caused by the waves.

When we left our home our floors were only about fourteen inches under water, but others around us reported of their homes being four feet and more in freezing water. This seemed horrendous at the time of our perilous journey to safety but later we met people who had experienced water up as high as their ceilings.

I remember looking down enviously from the top deck of the bus at three children being rowed away from their home in a small boat. "How exciting," I thought, not recognising the full sense of danger involved. It seemed of little importance to a twelve year old when my mother complained, "Things will never get dried out. All the walls are soaked through."

Our first stop on the mainland was another school. It was the local grammar school and this was the closest I was going to get to seeing inside one! Here we were served tea and sandwiches by generous local helpers. Each time more evacuees were brought into the large school hall people scanned the newcomers for friends and relatives. There were many tearful reunions, and also tales of tragedy.

Several members of my family, including one of my grandmothers, spent many hours on the roof of their homes awaiting rescue in the cold gale-stricken night. But even this ordeal was later retold with touches of humour. One woman told how her family had scrambled onto the roof of their outhouse. As the flood waters flowed past she saw a nice chair trapped in bushes in her garden. "Jim, that will go nicely in the front room. Go and get it." Jim bravely clambered down into the icy water to rescue the chair, and dragged it back onto the roof. His wife complained, "That's no bloody good, Jim, it's only got three legs. Chuck it back."

One fireman later told how he and my father rowed a boat to a bungalow to rescue an elderly couple only to be told, "Come back in half an hour, we're just having a cup of tea." And in another similar incident a woman refused to get into the boat until she had scrambled back into the house to change her knickers.

My family was finally evacuated to Harold Hill, Essex, on the outskirts of London where kindly people made it possible for my immediate family to stay together, although at that time we had no idea of the whereabouts of my father, and worried for his safety. We learned later that my father was safe and, fortunately also the rest of our family, but in the meantime we spent many hours in tears and dazed uncertainty.

On Monday 2 February 1953, the Prime Minister, Winston Churchill, rose before a packed House of Commons and said, "The disaster which has fallen on the inhabitants of Canvey Island seems to have been a most grievous one". This was a considerable understatement, although at that time the full extent of people missing, the human suffering, and loss of property was not yet known.

People were shocked into awakening by cold water and floating furniture bumping around their homes.

54

People clambered onto roofs and into lofts, soaking wet and icy cold as the wind continued to lash the coast and add to the misery they faced.

For hours mothers clung to young children trying desperately to fight off the dangerous effect of extreme exposure. Old people drew on hidden reserves of energy to clamber onto rooftops and clung together to await rescue. Only when day broke was the full enormity of the disaster more apparent. It was now possible to have a clearer idea of the full extent of the tragedy that was unfolding.

My father was employed by the Ford Motor Company at the time of the floods, and they were wonderful. They did much to ensure that we were clothed and suffered minimum hardship. They sent a chauffeur-driven car to take us to a department store to choose new clothes and other necessities. Many other firms also gave generously to help the evacuees. And contributions to a disaster fund came in from all over the world.

Residents were discouraged from returning to their homes before the authorities were sure that the defences were secure. This could not be assured until after the spring tides had passed — about the 19 February, almost three weeks after the momentous break in the sea wall.

Whilst an important priority for the flooded island was to repair the sea wall to prevent further flooding, this had the adverse effect of retaining flood waters already within the wall. This had to be removed. This was partly achieved by the existing tidal sluices and extra new ones that had been hastily created during the deluge, but a considerable volume of flood water remained lying in hollows. This was channelled towards the island's network of ditches by digging trenches and the operation of pumps manned by council workers and the local volunteer fire brigade.

An amazing sight awaited those returning to the island. Quite apart from the apparent physical devastation caused by the floodwater, there was a frantic workforce of military and civil personnel everywhere. It was not unusual to see a large amphibious Army vehicle (DUKW) trundling along the only highway that existed at that time. The scene was reminiscent of wartime when services moved into an area suffering from bomb damage, trying to salvage what was worth saving.

The RAF had brought in bomber engine heaters to blow dry damp homes, leaving a white line of salt on inside walls as a reminder of the level the sea water had reached. These heaters were fondly called "Windy Willies" by the RAF, but were soon christened "Chestnut Roasters" by the grateful local community. They were painted blue and had a huge green hose that snaked from the heater on the street into the house being treated.

Operation "Mrs Mop" was the name given to the mop-up operation provided mainly by volunteers to help the elderly, the disabled, and the sick to make their homes habitable. The volunteer organisations such as the WRVS and the Salvation Army were prominent in the operation, but this was also where young people showed how they could contribute to the community spirit when given the opportunity to do so.

At this time I was a member of the Boy Scouts. Our scout leader decided that our troop should join the mop-up operation, and he played an important role in coordinating the use of the various youth movements with the other voluntary organisations. At one time there were 823 scouts and guides working with the adult teams providing for the needy of Canvey.

I participated enthusiastically in the scheme, although there were difficulties. A minor problem for me was that we were told to wear our scout's uniform while assisting the needy, so that we could be recognised as genuine helpers. This ruling made it difficult to do the dirty work involved and remain smart.

The sort of tasks we undertook were many and varied, and included general floor cleaning, washing curtains, repairing household gadgets and tools, and painting. Many houses had river silt and dampness in every room, and sometimes dead animals as well. The tasks involved were often too taxing for young boys such as me, but this was the harsh reality faced by returning residents.

A key factor in reclaiming homes from the filth of flood water and sewage was the almost unlimited supply of free disinfectant provided by the Ministry of Housing. The fact that it was free ensured that residents used it profusely and, therefore, it made a valuable contribution to the prevention of disease and as a cure for the mould and mildew created by the dampness in the homes.

A welcome contribution to the re-establishment of our homes was the free issue of ex-army spring beds and Australian-made woollen blankets, the labels of which clearly showed they were manufactured in the 1940s for war use. The quality of these items was outstanding, and much appreciated by those who had lost so much during the devastation.

In those days many families didn't own a washing machine. In our home, washing was done using a large gas-fired boiler, but this was inadequate for the volume of washing that was needed to be done in order to make our home habitable again. However, a major washing machine manufacturing company installed washing machines in the local British Legion hall to set up a laundry operated by volunteers. And an army mobile laundry was also placed at the disposal of the island.

Throughout Britain many companies rallied round to aid recovery from the major disaster that had hit the east coast with such devastating effect. From around the world caring people and governments sent helpers, money, food, blankets and other items to help the flood victims to rebuild their lives. This wonderful help was gratefully received because at that time many insurance companies refused to compensate for flood damage, blaming it on an "Act of God". So, God got the blame and the insurance companies got off lightly.

Quite apart from the devastating loss of lives and damage to property, adding to the sad homecoming for many people was the realisation that during their absence they had been burgled by criminal opportunists. These, the lowest of human flotsam of society, caused as much distress to many returning residents as they had experienced when being forced to leave their homes. Some people collapsed from shock and hysteria after seeing the state of the homes they had returned to, and for some the distress of burglary was the last straw.

One of our neighbours never recovered from the trauma of floods and the burglary of his home and he committed suicide some time later. But, of course, his death never appeared in the official statistics of loss of life as a result of the floods, nor was there any statistic that could measure the long-term distress that his wife was left with.

Fifty-nine people of Canvey Island died in the floods. When I returned to my school it was sad to learn of the death of some of the children we had known. One boy who had drowned was the strongest swimmer in my group of friends. Another of my classmates had lost three of his brothers through drowning during the flood. What does one say to such friends? Some school friends just never returned to the island.

Today, of course, a tragedy of the scale of the floods of 1953 would be followed by trauma counselling. In those days this luxury was non-existent, and the thought of such needs did not enter our heads. Even those who had lost loved ones just had to pick up the pieces and get on with their lives as best as possible.

The media did much to help young people like myself to come to terms with the trauma of the floods.

They gave explanations and posed questions to help us understand the drama that had taken place. But sometimes the media does not get the response it expects to questions it puts. Teachers are used to this, but the media is sometimes taken by surprise, especially when it's a "live" interview.

I was listening to one such live broadcast when the interviewer asked a child the innocuous question, "What causes the sea tides?" The child seriously replied, "The tides are a fight between the Earth and the Moon. All water flows towards the Moon because there is no water there. I forget where the sun joins this fight, but it does!" The interviewer seemed thrown by this statement, but it made good sense to me as a child at that time.

There was an encouraging outcome of the floods for me personally. When we were forced to leave our home by the rising water I was distressed at having to leave my cat clinging to the roof of our garden shed, and in due course I had to assume that he had drowned as so many other animals had. One evening, a few weeks after we had returned to our home, I was watching a children's programme on our little black and white television. The programme was highlighting the number of animals rescued during the floods and being held in an animal sanctuary, some twenty miles from my home and awaiting recovery. I was convinced that I saw my cat on the small, indistinct screen. My parents protested that I couldn't possibly recognise my cat from the poor picture on our television. I was adamant that I was right, but twenty miles was a long way away as far as I was concerned, and my parents didn't own a car. Fortunately, an elderly neighbour sympathised with me and drove me to the sanctuary. You can imagine my happiness when I found my cat, and he clearly recognised and was pleased to see me also.

CHAPTER
THREE

DEAD MAN'S BAY

My father was extremely bright in his youth. He passed the examination to go to grammar school. Later he also passed the examination to gain entry to a technical college. He was, unfortunately, unable to take advantage of either opportunity because his family could afford neither the clothing nor equipment needed, and it was a priority that, as the eldest son, he should get out to work as soon as possible to help support his mother and father and their large struggling family. Not surprisingly, the examination for entry to a grammar school featured importantly in my father's aspirations for me.

When the time for sitting the grammar school entrance examination (the Eleven-Plus) arrived, my father stressed the importance of it to my future. I did not put too much emphasis on it, however. I was in the top class of my junior school, and was invariably in the top three places for each of the main subjects. I now realise that my main weakness was that I saw the most important way to demonstrate my excellence was to show that I could complete any work set before anyone else.

Consequently, I inevitably committed careless errors, and this was to be my downfall.

I didn't gain a straight pass into the grammar school but ended up in a "pool" of near-miss candidates. We were all subsequently interviewed at the local education office by a panel to select those who would be accepted for the few remaining places. My father came to the interview with me, and afterwards I could tell he was disappointed in my performance and my apparent lack of recognition of the importance of the event. I was not successful and was destined to attend our only local secondary school. The reputation of this school, at that time, was far from good.

The school buildings were very ancient. Like all buildings on Canvey Island then, it was built of a very light structure, almost like a temporary building. It looked very much like a great big sprawling bungalow. It would have looked more at home in the outback of the Australian bush. But it was to be my place of education until I was fifteen and old enough to go out into the wide world of work.

I returned from hop picking to make the transfer from the junior to the secondary school much later than my classmates. Not only was I faced with a much larger and far rougher school, but I was also four weeks behind the lessons of other pupils. The headmaster was also new to the school. His predecessor had left the school in a cloud of shame. He had been caught pinching ladies underwear, sometimes off clothes lines, and, supposedly, sometimes while they were still wearing it! The story of his departure featured in detail in the newspapers that exploited that sort of thing. The new head was focused on changing the regime of the school and improving its image. He certainly had an uphill struggle ahead.

The first thing the new head did was to ban jeans and T-shirts, which were all the rage at that time, when so many teenagers were aping the young tragic film star, James Dean. It was a far cry from imposing a school uniform, but for our little, one secondary school island it was revolutionary. There was a big outcry from pupils and parents alike, but the new head won the day amidst a flood of publicity and public protestations.

The first time I went into the dining room of my new school the difference compared to my previous school was obvious. It was far larger, and much noisier. In fact, the noise was so great that it disturbed the headmaster in his study and he came charging in ringing a hand bell and hollering his head off. Once he had our complete attention he told us to put our lips closely together. He then delivered a magical statement. He said, "You will all sit there in silence and eat your lunch in silence, without opening your mouth once."

It has been said that the school years are the happiest days of your life, but I can't say that this was honestly so for me. My new secondary school was, in my view, a dismal place where expectations were not high, and bullying was all too often raising its ugly head.

The school was certainly a rough one, as one might expect with so many of its pupils drawn from the families of wartime emigrants from London. Like all youngsters transferring from junior to secondary school, I found the older boys big and intimidating. Even pupils just one year older than us took delight in exacting on the newcomers the bullying tactics that they had suffered the year before.

I found the bullying aspect of school disturbing, as most civilised young people do. I witnessed some very sad cases of bullying, and no one did anything about it. The obvious targets were the weak and vulnerable and their lives were made a misery. When we went to the cinema to watch our favourite cowboy films, there was always a hero who took on the bullies and sorted them out. But I saw no heroes at our school.

I had to follow a route home from school which took me in the vicinity of elder twin boys. No matter which route I took they were waiting for me and many fights took place. I wore National Health Service spectacles and so many pairs got broken that my parents were warned that, unless I took "more care" of them, future replacements would have to be paid for. My father used to tell me to remember, "Sticks and stones may break my bones but names will never hurt me". But remembering this didn't help to stop my glasses getting broken.

Physical education lessons were noticeably far more strenuous than they had been in the junior school. Gone were bean bags, hoops and skipping ropes, and in came far more demanding activities, including long-distance runs around the roads of the island. In those days it was possible to take out a class of pupils running on the main road without fear of a few of them being killed or abducted by passing motorists.

One of the routes for the regular road runs involved two circuits of a collection of streets, one of which conveniently passed very close to my home. I and two friends would ensure we dragged along as the very last of the queue of runners and, once those in front had turned a corner with the teacher in the lead, we would dash into my home for a cup of tea. Then, as the column passed on the second circuit, we would tag on to the end. So, we were always the last ones to arrive in the changing rooms.

My dismal performance on these runs must have given the impression that I was useless at running, but this was far from the case. I had an older friend who was a serious runner who trained several times a week. I had a crush on his younger sister and in order to have an excuse to visit their home, I would do hard, long-distance runs with him. Consequently, it was quite a shock to everyone when I ran home in first place of the three mile race in the annual sports.

On one class run, along with two friends, we actually tagged along on the whole course, but at the end of the line of course. The three of us were playing "tail end Charlie", as usual, when we found we were being trailed by a decrepit-looking man on an old bike. He started trying to chat to us, offering us a shilling to pee in a bottle. My immediate reaction was to tell him to clear off, but one of our friends was more astute. He suggested that we meet him after school in one of the fields. Later we reported our assignation to the teacher and the police were informed.

The "dirty" old man was caught and we were paraded in the next school assembly as heroes. Our only female friend, Laura, said, we were "Idjits" because she would rather have had the shilling, and it was a cruel trick to play on someone so generous. Mind you, Laura was also generous to those who could afford her charms, but as I hadn't started a paper round yet I did not manage to get that close to her.

I couldn't rake up any interest in Laura. A couple of my friends talked of times they had taken her over the fields and got to see her knickers for pennies, and more for a shilling (5p). I guess I hadn't matured enough to want to spend my meagre pocket money in this way.

My favourite teacher was a huge man who taught geography and ruled with an iron fist. If you messed around in most teachers' lessons you were rewarded with a carefully aimed piece of chalk. In Mr Gregory's case the blackboard rubber was his favourite missile. But I enjoyed his lessons because of the strong discipline he imposed. It was possible to learn in his classroom. He taught me about the weather. For example he once stated that my hair looked as if it had passed through a hurricane. He also taught me logic. He used to say, "Because I said so, boy, that's why."

One of the strange differences between the junior and the secondary school was that, although boys and girls shared classes, we were separated at break times. Within a year of his appointment the new head decided we should integrate, which was a lot more fun. In fact, my friend David declared that it was much better being bisexual!

Probably the most difficult subject to teach in the school was religion. The teacher of this subject was very ineffectual, and he didn't have much chance considering the attitude of most of the pupils when I joined the school. It was really my Mum that taught me religion. She used to say, "You'd better pray to God that stain will come out of those trousers." She also taught me contortionism by telling me, "Will you just look at the dirt on the back of your neck?"

I found I got on well with most of my teachers, but one of them terrified all of the youngsters, even the bullies. I became very apprehensive in his lessons and my mind went blank as soon as he asked me a question. One day when he was getting a bit frustrated with my hesitant answers to his questions, he asked, "What's your name, boy?" "It's Alan Whitcomb, Sir," I replied. "My God, your memory is not as bad as it appears. Can't you remember at least something I have taught you?" Needless to say, I never found his subject inspiring.

I quite liked learning mathematics at school, but I hit a crisis point in the subject at a crucial stage of my learning. When I was about twelve years of age I got a bit hooked on jazz, traditional jazz, in particular. I heard a few well known groups play live, and several local amateur groups, that were more fun in their improvisation. I got to thinking that I would like to play the trumpet. I couldn't afford a trumpet or lessons, so I joined the Salvation Army.

If I attended their Sunday school I could also join their music group, where they provided the instruments

68

and the tuition, which took place once a week. We were allowed to take the instruments home to practice the pieces we were learning. And I was not going to have to wear the uniform until I could play. This was going to take some time, I was sure.

The music wasn't jazz of course, far from it. But my theory was that if I learnt music and had access to a trumpet, I could play their music in lessons and experiment with jazz at home. The lessons went quite well and my versions of a very slow "Abide With Me" and "Basin Street Blues" did arouse my family and neighbours, although not with enthusiasm I must admit.

My problem with mathematics arose when I started to learn fractions at the same time as I was learning in music to count beats. I became totally confused. For example, for some reason my brain couldn't cope with three four time and three quarters. The problem became so bad for me that I had to abandon my budding jazz career.

Many years later, when in the Merchant Navy, I bought a trombone when my interest in jazz resurfaced. But that wasn't too successful either. My cabin mates banned me to the open deck to practice, but even there the noise was so painful that I received complaints about disturbing the first-class passengers on the lounge deck downwind from me. I just wasn't meant to be a jazz musician, I guess.

Following my Salvation Army period and the abandonment of my budding jazz career, someone told me that the voice is considered to be an instrument of music. They hadn't heard my voice of course, but it influenced me to join the local Church of England choir. I must admit the prospect of a little pocket money from singing at weddings had some influence. The height of excitement I enjoyed as a choir boy was when one of the lads sneaked some of his parents' vodka into the communion wine. We all thought we were going to see parishioners rolling in the aisle, but of course the effect of such a small amount was not noticeable. However, the excitement of the anticipation was delicious.

My best friend in the choir was a lad called Chris. Unlike me, he had a marvellous singing voice. But his knowledge of the Bible was sketchy to say the least. He persistently insisted that his favourite story from the Bible was the one about Jesus and the twelve bicycles. But, then again, he was also there for the pocket money.

In spite of the fact that I spent some time attending the Salvation Army Sunday school, and later spent a couple of years as a Church of England choir boy, I found it increasingly difficult to feel an affinity with any religion as I matured. This was not really caused by being disillusioned with religious precepts, but more because I found it difficult to dissociate religions from manipulation of the working man, and women in particular.

It seemed to me it was a point of faith that men were seen as the direct descendants of the lords of creation, and women were of secondary consideration, not withstanding the fact that many men are undeserving of such reverence. Indeed, even some male religious leaders were found to be wanting in moral standards. One of our local vicars at that time was prosecuted for interfering with young boys. Is it any wonder that women increasingly questioned the deference accorded to men in the past as miniatures of the exacting, all-powerful, all forgiving God whom they worshipped?

Two new boys joined our school. Although they were both older than me, I quickly became friends with them through our membership of the Boy Scouts. Ted had moved to Canvey Island from Poplar in London. Ted told me one day that he was circumcised. I told him I thought that was great as I wanted to join a circus one day! Horst arrived from Hanover in Germany. They each had contrasting tales to tell of their experiences during the war years.

Ted, like so many London children, had been evacuated away from an area likely to be bombed. He was sent to far away South Wales, a place that few young Londoners had ever expected to visit. He was allocated to a Mr Evans, a bachelor farmer who wanted a boy to help around the farm.

Farmer Evans was a scraggy, red-haired man with no compassion, and Ted referred to him as "Evans the Red". He used Ted as a skivvy, collecting eggs, feeding the pigs, and mucking out the stables. He gave little in return.

Ted was allowed in the farmhouse once a day to sit in the kitchen late at night to eat his only meal of stew and dry bread. During the day he would forage for berries and anything else he could find to eat. At night he slept in a hay barn with one filthy blanket that smelt of horses. He washed out in the open from a standpipe.

Ted was woken early in the morning with a prod from Farmer Evans' boot, and a gruff command of, "Get up yer lazy tyke" and set to work on an empty stomach. One day Evans found Ted gnawing on a piece of turnip meant to be fed to the pigs. He was given a thrashing to add to his starved belly.

But Ted took great glee in telling how the wife of one of Farmers Evans' neighbours wrote to inform his mother of his ill-treatment. His mother travelled all the way from London to Wales, gave Farmer Evans a good thumping, and took Ted home. The danger of the blitz was deemed less menacing than the ill-treatment from "Evans the Red".

Horst's wartime experience was traumatic in a different way, but the final outcome was as equally satisfying as Ted's. Towards the end of the war Horst and his mother learnt that Horst's father had been killed while serving in the German army on the Russian front. Times were hard for the two of them, and food was in short supply. Then a British Tommy, from Canvey, discovered their plight. He brought them food and helped them to maintain their simple home in whatever way he could. In due course he brought Horst and his mother to England, where he married the mother and, I assume, they all lived happily ever after.

I found Horst's accent fascinating and some of the things he said, and the way that he said them, amusing. The fact that his stepfather had a strong Irish brogue probably didn't help matters much. He had a good grasp of English which was coloured with bits of Cockney slang we had taught him and tinted with a mixture of Irish and German accents.

Neither Ted nor Horst were really badly scarred by their experiences but Horst loved everything about England, whereas Ted was left with deep-felt anti-Welsh tendencies.

Boys at school were always trying to out-do each other with bragging. I actually believed them when two lads told me that they had got in to see an adult movie at the local cinema by telling the cashier they were midgets! Another brag that was often made, a true one in fact, was that several boys would pool their resources to pay for one person who would go into the cinema, he would then creep to the emergency exit and open it from the inside to let the rest of the gang in free.

A long lasting school memory for me, particularly in these days of non-corporal punishment, is that of a diminutive lady teacher knocking hells bells out of a large boy who she caught letting down the tyres of her bicycle. There was a large crowd of us cheering her on as she hit him with some mighty blows. Even the boy saw the funny side of it all and readily pumped up her tyres again.

For really serious misdemeanours the culprit could be caned on the school stage in front of the whole school during morning assembly. On one such occasion, the biggest boy in the school was the culprit. He stood on the stage and dwarfed the senior teachers there. The headmaster gave his spiel about, "This will hurt me more than it will hurt you." The young giant obviously didn't believe this because he refused to put out his hand to accept the punishment. There was deadly silence while everyone waited to see how the head would deal with the situation. Then one of the lads called out, "coward", and the giant meekly stretched out his hand and took the two strokes. I think the head must have silently blessed the boy who called out and saved an embarrassing situation. Caning in assemblies stopped after that incident, but the caning continued in the privacy of the Head's study.

I was to receive a caning on one occasion. A friend of mine was caught smoking in the outside toilets and taken to the headmaster for punishment. He, for some reason, told the head that the cigarettes were mine. When I was summoned to the head's study. I denied this. I was caned twice, once, for bringing cigarettes to school, and a second for lying. Unjust though this punishment was, I do not think it did me any harm, and I still feel that corporal punishment is acceptable in some circumstances.

Although our secondary education did not lead to any formal public examinations, we sat internal examinations and tests towards the end of each academic year. These were particularly used to help the teachers to write our end of year reports.

Unfortunately for some, our teachers would cruelly read out some of the answers we had written in the examinations. For example, in answer to the geography question, "Name the four seasons", one lad had written, "Salt, vinegar, mustard, pepper". Now I consider that creative thinking rather than a reason for ridicule. I thought another good answer was given to the question, "What is a planet?" Surely, this answer, "A body of earth surrounded by sky", was pure genius in the class of Einstein?

At the end of each academic year we received our reports. This was a time of apprehension for me because I was anxious to please my parents following my failure during the Eleven-Plus fiasco. Usually the contents of my reports were reasonably favourable, and the most critical comment I justly received was, "Always first with the answers, but not always correct." I was always heartened by the knowledge that Albert Einstein's school report stated, "He will never amount to anything"!

I always took my report home unopened and in the ominous brown envelope it was sealed in. But many of my friends opened their reports and took great joy in reading out some of the caustic comments to anyone who would listen to them. The contents of my friend David's report was widely circulated one year, and it included the following gems:

English: If David applied half the time and effort to his English studies that he puts into acting the fool he could dispel the impression that he is a complete idiot.
Science: David suffers from a distorted sense of humour. This can be very dangerous in the laboratory.
Physical Education: I suspect that David either

has glue in his plimsolls, or he is extraordinarily
lazy.

Head Teacher's comments: David seems to think
he is running this school and not me. Unless
he changes his opinion one of us will have to
leave.

During the summer holidays some of my family's
former friends from London would take turns to come
and visit us. In the summer of my first year at
secondary school a couple of my parent's friends visited
with their two sons, who were of a similar age to me. I
had been looking forward to taking them across the
fields to where our gang had built a hideaway. But the
boys had never walked through long grass before; their
playground was the derelict bomb sites near where they
lived. As we walked through the grass they clearly
didn't like the feel of it whipping around their legs. All
the way across the fields they yelled with terror and
hopped from one foot to the other as if walking on hot
coals. To make matters worse, they were unused to
exposure to sun and they rapidly got sunburnt. Even
when we reached the hideaway they wouldn't go inside
in case there were spiders. I thought my former friends
from London had become wimps!

Once we were no longer going hop picking, autumn
and late September particularly, became an important
time of the year for me for another reason. I would go
out very early in the morning, before needing to leave
for school, to collect mushrooms in the fields near my
home. At this time of first light, thick mist lay like

foaming milk across the fields which were so close to the River Thames. Sometimes other mushroom collectors could be seen eerily disembodied by the mist as we competed with each other for the harvest that had grown since the previous day.

Having collected my haul of free mushrooms I would get on my bike and take them to one of the several local greengrocers who were setting up their display for the day's trade. They would give me 25 per cent of what they would sell the mushrooms for. I would then race home to get ready to leave for school.

At the weekend, when there was no need to go to school, I would sell my mushrooms direct to holiday-makers on the local caravan site, charging them half the price they would have to pay the greengrocer, this doubled my income by cutting out the middleman. My budding entrepreneurial skills were beginning to show.

I was furious one day when I was out mushroom picking in my usual spot. Two buses suddenly arrived and stopped by the field. Two men and two women, in uniforms, jumped off the buses (they had drivers and conductors in those days) and dashed into "my" field. They ran around for ten minutes gathering "my" crop, and then shot back to their buses and drove off. Is it any wonder that we wait for ages for a bus, and then two turn up together?

"Gangs" featured high in the priorities of young south Essex teenagers, and everyone wanted to belong to one. These groups were neither sinister nor disruptive at that time. Our gang consisted only of boys, about a dozen, of varying ages and we all attended the same school. Our escapades included innocent activities such as our own team for football, cricket and rounders, go-cart production, field camps, bonfire building, and swimming contests. None of our activities harassed the local community. Vandalism was against our rules and graffiti was not familiar to us. Probably the only thing that we did that could be regarded in any way anti-social was scrumping.

Scrumping was really a "no go" area for me, much to the disgust of my friends who thought I was a bit of a wimp in this respect. Although scrumping was seemingly accepted while hop picking, it certainly wasn't accepted in my home neighbourhood. The problem was that my father was a local Justice of the Peace, and I took very seriously the threat of punishment if I brought shame on the family name.

In reality scrumping was an unnecessary devilment because there was no need to steal fruit. Most of the homes had some form of fruit tree in their gardens, and a knock on a door with a request to collect "windfalls" was invariably granted. But scrumping was part of the gang culture of that time. However, certainly scrumping seems quite innocuous compared with some of the antics that youths seem to get up to in modern times.

Our nearest competing gang existed just half a dozen streets away. They were known as the "Jones Mob", after the name of their oldest member. We were the "Southwick Rovers", after the biggest road we all lived near. Further away was another gang called "The

Council House Wallas", who lived on the newly built council estate not far away from our area.

Regular competing events took place between the gangs; these included rounders, cricket, and football matches, and many others which we had devised ourselves. These were highly competitive but never aggressive. No referee was needed. We all acknowledged the rules, even though many of them were our own. The Southwick Rovers goalkeeper went on to play professional in goal for West Ham United, probably due entirely to the excellent preparation we gave him! He certainly couldn't have had a tougher introduction to the sport.

Fireworks night was an important event for both gangs and, prior to 5 November, we would compete to see who could build the biggest bonfire in the nearby fields. There was the usual assortment of rubbish and old furniture that our families and neighbours wanted to dispose of, but we needed to search further to compete with our rival gang. The next source of material was shrubs and trees — the bigger the better.

The fields of Canvey Island were drained by a network of dykes or ditches. The dykes that were alongside the roads were maintained by the local council, and those in the fields were kept clear by the farmers. The dykes invariably contained bushes and brambles, and no one objected to us cutting these down for our bonfire as we were helping to keep the dykes from becoming overgrown.

One year, when bonfire building had become particularly competitive, we had a brainwave. We went round houses knocking on doors and offering to "prune" trees and shrubs and take away the cuttings completely free of charge. The idea being that we would obtain "meatier" logs in this way.

We arrived at one house, armed with such an array of saws and axes and dishevelled clothing that I'm sure that we looked more like pirates than tree surgeons in short trousers. However, the lady of the house seemed to take our "tree pruners" waffle quite seriously and gave us most elaborate instructions of where she wanted cuts made, and which parts of the large fruit tree should not be touched under any circumstances.

We gaily went to work with blissful abandon, oblivious to any instructions and hideously mutilated the poor tree. I'm sure that one of our heroes, Robin Hood, would have been so disappointed in our disrespect for trees. The poor lady was horrified, and she chased us up the road for a long way hurling abuse at us. I hate to imagine how she explained it all to her husband when he came home from work. But what else can you really expect from a free service by budding butchers?

Together with my brother and sister, one day we made a guy with a shirt and a suit stuffed with newspapers, and topped with a very neat trilby hat that we found hanging on a hook just inside the British Legion hall. We stood with our guy in a homemade barrow outside the local grocery shop on the main road, asking for, "a penny for the guy". We were given a few coppers, but not enough to buy more than a single firework.

Some people commented that our guy did not look very realistic. This was a bit harsh considering that it was our Dad's suit it was wearing, and he hadn't actually finished wearing it at the time. But it did cause us to consider how we could improve the image of our guy. We decided that I would dress up in the clothes, pad me out with newspapers, put a sacking bag over my head and don the guy's mask.

I was wheeled round to the shop, but still people complained that our guy was not very realistic. I mean how more realistic can you get than a real body! The final straw came when one old lady prodded me viciously with her umbrella and nearly had a heart attacked when I let out a scream of pain.

There was a time close to the big day when we had to guard our bonfire until late at night to protect our treasured heap from marauding raids by other gangs. When 5 November arrived, the early evening after school was spent in anxious preparation for the lighting of the fire. The bonfire was stuffed with as many newspapers as possible to ensure a good start to the flames, and prayers were cast aloft to keep the rain away. One of the last of the preparations was to hoist the several guys we had each made to a high position on the bonfire. This was no mean task considering how high the bonfire had become, and the unstable nature of its structure.

Once it was dark the gang would congregate around the bonfire, together with their families and neighbours. Really anybody was welcomed to the fire, so long as they had a respectable collection of fireworks to bring along. A few families would really get into the swing of things and bring along some delicacies, such as cheese and onion sandwiches.

When the fire was successfully burning with showers of sparks flying everywhere, groups would take turns in setting off some of their fireworks and the night sky was lit up by rockets not only from our gathering, but also by those in other fields and gardens. We were fortunate that none of the farmers objected to our invasion of their fields, or the debris that remained after the event.

Guy Fawke's Night was not one that my father could relax and enjoy. As a local volunteer fireman he knew that he was sure to be called out at some time during the night, and his bicycle would stand ready for his sprint to the fire station when the siren sounded. I was once told in a geography lesson in school that they sometimes deliberately start fires in Australia to burn the bush and replenish the land. Well we certainly cleared some areas on bonfire night, but I don't think our fires helped to replenish the land.

During the warm sunny days of summer many of us made our way to the beach after school as often as possible. A few lads were fortunate to have boats or canoes. I was lucky that one of my friends acquired a canoe that we had a lot of fun with in the safety of a back creek. I was very taken with the idea of messing about in the canoe and my friend offered to get me a second hand one from his "source" for the princely sum of £1 10s. A deal was agreed and in due course my friend and his brother carried a canoe in excellent condition, complete with paddles, into my back garden.

I was now the proud owner of my own canoe. Well I was until my father arrived home from work. He realized straight away that it must have been stolen to be so cheap. I was made to go with my friend and carry it back to its original mooring in the creek. And as a punishment to me, my friend was to be allowed to keep the money I had paid him.

Our regular swimming place was officially called Thorney Bay, but it was usually referred to by locals as "Dead Man's Bay". This is a small bay that is part of the River Thames, and where for many years the bodies of people who had drowned in the river had been trapped and washed ashore by the tidal flow. Hence, the nickname "Dead Man's Bay".

In spite of its ominous nickname the bay was popular because it provided an ideal site for improvised swimming contests. At its widest point at the mouth, it was only about 300 yards across, and inshore the width became progressively narrower. It was also relatively shallow, so swimmers of varying stages of proficiency could choose an appropriate place to swim from one side of the bay to the other in relative safety.

On one of our swimming expeditions a few of us boys decided that we would see who could swim furthest underwater. Our judge was to be a girl from our year group who had started to hang around with us. Although she was not pretty, she was accepted because one of the boys reckoned she was one of the first girls in our year group to have the beginnings of "boobs" appearing. I thought she was just a bit fat!

We took turns to dive into the murky sea, while our judge made a mental note of where we broke the surface. I was to be the last to go. Diving and swimming underwater was not within my category of experience; I had only just graduated to swimming without putting my foot down to make sure I wasn't out of my depth. However, I concluded that if I could dive low enough, hold my breath hard, and kick and wave my hands about as much as possible I could make a reasonable showing.

I dived off of the breakwater, pushing down as deep as possible. All of a sudden there was an explosion in both of my ears. I felt a pain in each ear that seemed to stretch down to my throat. The intense pain continued as I made my way to the shore, where the others were arguing heatedly about who had remained below the surface the longest. I no longer cared; I was still in considerable pain.

A few weeks later I noticed, when listening to my watch tick that I couldn't hear it as well in one ear as the other. Later it became clear that both of my ears were deteriorating. I was also experiencing a smelly discharge from both ears.

Initially my doctor prescribed drops to clear up the discharge. But in due course a session with a hospital specialist confirmed that I had perforated both ear drums. This was the beginning of a hearing loss that was to become progressively worse and have a profound effect on my future life.

In spite of going through ten operations on my ears, my hearing loss has continued to decline and today I cannot exist without the help of two hearing aids. Although my hearing loss has placed many limitations on my life, it has, surprisingly enough, favourably affected my personal development. It has made me determined to succeed despite this handicap.

During the last year at the secondary school, we were treated to a short course of sex education. For me it was probably too short, and for some of my friends it was too late. Nobody actually "talked" to us, but we were shown several short films, from which I only remembered that every woman has a "volvo", but the Volvo was not a well known car at that time!

The girls had separate sex education from us boys. Laura told us something about their programme, although she assured us that it was nothing new to her, and it probably wasn't. Laura explained to us that men and women made love when there was an "election", but she couldn't explain how that decided whether there would be a Labour or a Conservative government. She told us that one of their films was about periods, but I was none the wiser. However, I did hope that from a combination of our films, and Laura's graphic reports, if I eventually got a girlfriend, I might remember enough to have some idea what to do. Wrong!

During my last year at secondary school we received very little career guidance. In a vague careers interview with a teacher I said I wanted to draw advertisements, because I was fairly good at art. But I was told that I wouldn't be able to do this because I was left-handed.

My father wasn't particularly disturbed by this because he couldn't see a future for me in art.

My second careers interview was to be with the local careers officer. As this was viewed as a key step for my future, my father was to accompany me. My father was an engineer and wanted me to go into engineering also, but I wasn't at all keen on this. Knowing my advertising career was a dead duck, we reached a happy compromise. I would become a draftsman.

We attended our joint interview and explained to the careers officer my new ambition. He said it was unlikely that I would be successful because I was "left-handed". This left-handed business was becoming a bit of a pain, and it was from here on that I decided I would eventually like to join the Merchant Navy and see the world as soon as I was old enough, assuming there was such a thing as a left-handed seaman.

CHAPTER
FOUR

AUSTRALIA BOUND

Quite apart from my disillusionment with school and education, I'm not sure that the early 1950s were particularly good for the wider population either. Notwithstanding the effects locally of the floods that took place, it was a grey time for the country generally and there was little to cheer about. Britain was at war with Korea, and later involved in conflict in Cyprus also. There was petrol rationing, and we could only win one gold medal at the Helsinki Olympics.

However, there were some golden moments for the 1950s. The Coronation, the first ascent of Everest, and Roger Banister breaking the four minute mile all gave Britain something to cheer about. Also England won back the Ashes, an event that has become increasingly rare.

Of course our political masters were always telling us how good things were, or how good they were going to become in the 1960s. North Sea oil was going to wipe out Britain's balance of payments problem, just like that, and it would change the whole economic climate of the country and make us rich again!

But, for me, even leaving school to go out to work couldn't stop me from feeling trapped in a life without a golden horizon, if there was such a thing. Although the majority of my childhood was spent close to the sea, there was limited opportunity to experience first-hand life aboard the ships, passing up and down the River Thames that I could see from my bedroom window.

The extent of my previous seaboard experiences had been the annual few minutes, ferry crossings between Tilbury and Gravesend on the way to the hop fields in Kent, and occasional trips from Southend Pier up the River Thames by paddle steamer to central London. On one momentous occasion I had been taken by my mother on a day trip to France by ship. These brief experiences left me with a vision of a ship as a breathing thing.

Having left school with no qualifications at the age of fifteen, I worked for a short time in the offices of a London shipping agent as a messenger, travelling from Essex into London and back each day — which cost a third of my wages. In my work I would deliver and collect freight documents, walking the streets of the eastern sector of the city. It was in this area of London where the head offices of many major shipping lines were to be found.

The windows of most shipping companies contained models of their vessels. The window displays that inspired me most were those of companies that owned passenger liners. Companies such as Cunard, Royal Mail, Canadian Pacific and the Orient Line displayed beautiful models; some also showed miniature cabins. One company even had a full-sized cabin on display in its foyer to entice potential passengers.

I spent far too long gazing longingly at the models in the windows, dreaming of far away places when I should have been hurrying to make a delivery or collection. I was often scolded when I returned to the office for taking so long to return. I invariably came up with my standard excuse that I had "got lost", but this excuse, used too often, began to be disbelieved.

Those windows and their displays fuelled the existing desire to go to sea that had developed towards the end of my school days. The thirst to go to sea may also have been encouraged by the sunny posters in the shipping companies' windows, showing bronzed young girls and telling me to "Come to Australia".

I reached the stage where I really couldn't take any more of the dead-end boredom of traipsing around London, delivering messages to save my employer's time and postage costs, not to mention having to continually pass the enticing shipping company windows extolling me to be anywhere else other than in London. I was young and restless; I wanted to go away to sea and visit places far away.

Like many other Essex youngsters, I saw a life in the Merchant Navy as a means of travelling the world. Certainly it was going to be better than wandering around the City, not to mention the boring travel to and from London each day.

The fate for the first five years of my working life was sealed by exciting stories from my uncle who was in the

Merchant Navy. I wanted to go to sea. I had serious discussions with my parents who, while not fully opposing my wish, wanted me to wait until I was older. Quite apart from this, they saw my office job as the final word in security.

All the literature I obtained about becoming a seaman told me that, for a boy below the age of eighteen, the pathway to life as a merchant seaman lay through one of the training schools. But the minimum age was sixteen years. In spite of the fact that, at age fifteen, I was underage, I decided to apply in the hope that I would be guaranteed a place for when I reached the age of sixteen.

I applied to the Merchant Navy and initially attended a medical examination. Although my hearing loss was not particularly obvious at this time, I was sure that the examination would reveal the perforations and eliminate me. But this was not the case. I was awarded a place at the training school at Gravesend in Kent in 1956. The application form asked for my date of birth but did not ask for age. Eventually I received a letter allocating me a place even though I was only part-way through my fifteenth year. I guessed that someone with a weak mathematical mind had assumed that with a birth date of 1940 applying in 1956, I must be sixteen years of age. I certainly had no intention of enlightening them and readily accepted the place.

The sea school was a rather depressing red-bricked building which housed about 150 boys. Some people said that it had in the distant past been a prison. It certainly had the appearance of a small prison on the inside. The dormitory floors contained small cell-like bedrooms with balconies, which surrounded a large open square, rather like those often featured in classic old films of prisons.

The literature from the training school assured the parents of applicants that the food and the training did wonders for the health of the boys, and claimed that all boys showed healthy weight gain during the six weeks of the training course. The main fare that sticks in my memory was the stodgy porridge made with water (and no sugar), and the thick slices of bread that we referred to as "dogs" for some reason. Certainly not appetising, but pleasingly filling! Sometimes, when there was an absence of margarine, we would sprinkle "dogs" with salt and pepper to give them some flavour so that we could eat them to help fill a grumbling tummy.

In retrospect I agree that the training was healthy, but I have doubts about the weight gain. The fare provided was basic and meagre and I doubt if I would have survived without periodic visits from my family with food parcels. However, I have always thought that the course provided a good experience and a sound introduction for a working life at sea. In fact, many of the lessons I learnt at the sea school have remained useful throughout my life, not least of all knowing when to keep your mouth shut.

There were two broad options for recruits. One was to take a course to become a deck hand, the other was for catering. I chose the latter because I felt that I would be learning skills that would be of use in later life. This was something that several adults had warned

I should consider. In reality I have never used the knowledge acquired in employment, although the social skills learned have often been useful.

The six week's course included the physical training and discipline one might expect in preparing young boys for a life requiring recognition of authority, and strict standards of dress and behaviour. The compulsory uniform and regular inspections did much to instil these requirements.

I was proud to wear the training cadets' uniform. One weekend I was returning to my home on Canvey Island and was impatient to get off the train. I stood up at the train door far too early in anticipation of the station. A man sitting near the door looked at the words "Merchant Navy" on the shoulders of my uniform and said, "You've got a bit of a way to go yet. It shows you've been away for some time." I had been away from home just two weeks, and less than twenty miles away. But it did my ego good that at fifteen years of age an adult thought I was worldly wise.

Square bashing was a daily feature of the training. We would be marched in full uniform to the nearby sea-front and manoeuvred around by the commands of our officers. During these exercises the catering trainees would compete against the deck trainees to execute the manoeuvres in the best manner. Just imagine the scene, with columns of brightly scrubbed lads marching up and down the parade ground in ill-fitting uniforms, trying to make their brightly polished shoes drum out a disciplined tattoo, with very limited success.

There were no official judges of these competitions except for a scattering of local girls, who came and watched, giggled, and gave come-hither looks to the recruit they fancied. Under the close watch of the officers it was difficult to make dates, but we managed to drop pieces of paper to be pounced on, hopefully by the right girl. For me this led to the briefest of romances, which was largely uneventful but perpetuated by shameful promises of the wondrous gifts I was going to return with from my wanderings.

"Jankers" was a feature of the discipline at the sea school. If you were found "out of bounds", such as in a pub or out of the school "after hours", "jankers" was imposed. For us, "jankers" meant not being allowed out of the training school for three days and nights. This was no great problem for me as I wasn't interested in drinking in pubs, and I had no money to contemplate any other forms of diversion.

An important part of our course was learning the terminology used on ships, particularly those that replaced the ones that had been common to us throughout our lives so far. So we began to refer to the floor as the deck, the ceiling as the deck head, stairs as companion ways, and the toilets as the "heads".

More difficult to grasp were the terms port and starboard, and the colours of the lights that accompanied these aspects of a ship. I managed to remember that port was the left side of the ship when looking forward. This knowledge was established in my brain by remembering that the word port contained the same number of letters as the word left. I also imagined the drink port being the same colour (red) as the port light of a ship. It was then easy to remember that the other side was starboard and green. Problem solved by a most devious route, but it worked for me.

Then, after six weeks' badgering from the officers responsible for our training, a miracle occurred. I realised that I really looked and acted the part. I certainly hadn't put on any weight, but my uniform certainly seemed to fit better — perhaps it had shrunk out in the rain. I was holding myself differently. I was more upright and confident.

What was supposed to be my first ship was a brand new vessel called the *Oronsay* which was embarking on one of its first voyages from Tilbury docks. My parents came with me to the railway station, and my father, who was only slightly bigger than my suitcase, insisted on carrying it up to the platform. We stood on the platform for a while in a silence occasionally interrupted by my mother's questions, "Have you packed . . .?"

It was a grey morning with a watery sun dripping its rays over Canvey Island. The sky held little promise for a bright day, and I was far from feeling bright myself. My iron resolve not to be emotional dissolved when I saw the tears in my mother's eyes. As the train approached the station, my father stammered, "Good luck, son." I shook his hand firmly and boarded the train quickly lest emotions got the better of me. I was only fifteen but I was making the bold move to self-sufficiency. I was nervous about what lay in store for me, but I honestly felt sure I was doing the right thing.

The train soon enough whisked me away from my anxious family towards the docks. At the dock gate I had to show my papers relating to the ship I was joining. "She's over there mate", the gatekeeper pointed, as if it were likely I could miss the directions to the 28,000 ton ocean liner that towered above all around her.

Climbing the crew gangway was like going up the side of a cliff. At the top of the gangway two officers sat behind desks, checking the crew as they came aboard. I signed on as an apprentice chef for her maiden voyage just hours before she was due to sail. I was to be paid the princely sum of £9 a month. In return for this measly payment I was required to work seven days a week, starting at seven in the morning and finishing at half past nine at night. Food and accommodation was free, but I had to provide all my own uniforms, the bill for which was £48. This seemed a very large debt to me at that time.

In order to reach my allocated cabin I had to follow a route along a maze of passages and down narrow companionways, frequently changing directions, until I reached the lower deck near the ship's water line, where the crew quarters were situated in the bowels of the ship.

The cabin where I was allocated a berth was a long narrow affair with six two-tier bunks on the right and four on the left. Beyond this there stood a row of metal lockers and a table with raised edges, like a tray, to stop things sliding off. The outer bulkhead had just two portholes letting dim light enter, and through these a glimmer of natural light was reflected from the sea that seemed all too close to the porthole. This small amount of natural light was supplemented by a few bare light bulbs that were almost permanently turned on.

As the last boy rating to arrive I took the only remaining bunk in the cabin. It had a couple of pillows, blankets and sheets piled on it. It was a top bunk and was so close to the deck head that there was little room to sit up. It was very claustrophobic, but little did I realise that this was not going to trouble me.

Unbeknown to me, many of my family had travelled to Tilbury Docks to wave goodbye. Then, minutes before the gangway was lowered, it was discovered that too many boy ratings had been signed on. It was decided that I should be the one to leave and join her sister ship, the considerably older *Orion*. The entire sixteenth year of my life was to be spent on the *Orion*, voyaging from England to Australia and up into the Pacific, and then back home again.

I left the *Oronsay* by the rear gangplank just as it was about to be removed, like the severing of the umbical chord between mother and child. At the same time my family waved a tearful goodbye among the crowds at the forward one. I walked with my suitcase to the less glamorous *Orion* in the next berth. I was so disappointed that I stowed my gear in my allocated cabin and caught the next train home. My family in the meantime had driven back to Canvey Island to repeat the farewell with tears on the sea wall as the *Oronsay* sailed past further down river. Eventually they all returned to my parent's home to commiserate, only to find me sitting there wondering where everyone was.

Life on the *Orion* was very new for me, and the first night I stayed onboard I found it difficult to sleep. I was the only person in the cabin and had no opportunity to become acquainted with my new cabin mates as they were all on shore leave. The constant hum of machinery and the air forced through the blowers were not restful. The off-white walls of the cabin and the two portholes that let in only nominal light ensured that the bulkhead lights were seemingly constantly on. During bad weather or emergencies, heavy metal plates called "dead lights" would be screwed down over the portholes, turning the cabin into a virtual iron box.

I "worked by" the *Orion* in the docks for two weeks, while my former ship, the *Oronsay*, sailed on into the sunshine of the Southern Ocean. In effect there was little work to do and I often went home at night to be with my family and journeyed to the ship each day. As the train on which I travelled drew near to the docks many masts, funnels and decks came into view, rather like a city, such was the busy life of Tilbury docks at that time. The *Orion's* corn coloured funnel with its black capping towered above the many cargo ships nearby, and beckoned crew members across the docks as she prepared to sail. The collection of vessels looked high and grand above the dockside sheds.

The *Orion* was built to accommodate two categories of passengers, first-class and tourist-class. The first-class passengers were accommodated in the main part of the vessel in sumptuous surroundings. These areas of the ship were superbly furnished, with lots of highly polished brass, massive mirrors at the top of wide sweeping staircases, and shiny corridors. Quiet areas were fitted with lush carpets. In the dining salon the stewards stood waiting attentively in their high buttoned jackets. The tables glittered with highly polished glass and silver.

I sometimes wondered if the first-class areas of the ship had been designed with the objective of keeping the passengers in an environment that hoodwinked them into thinking they were not on a ship at all — hardly the purpose of going on a sea cruise, it seemed to me! The first-class passengers were cocooned in an atmosphere of luxury that I had never experienced before, and I found it difficult to imagine that anyone could afford such opulence.

The tourist-class area, by contrast, was intended for those travelling at the most economical level, and the cabins, bars and dining salons were less impressive than the first-class, although far superior to the crew quarters of course.

The lower end of the tourist class social stratagem belonged to the emigrants, who were heading for Australia to start a new life, courtesy of a government assisted passage. This meant in effect that the emigrants had paid just £10 for their passage, with the remainder of their fare paid by the Australian government. In the case of their accommodation, six unrelated people shared a cabin. It was often the case that the husband would occupy a completely different cabin from that of his wife and children, although this could hardly be considered as hardship for the princely sum of £10!

The *Orion* eventually sailed, two weeks after I had joined her, and embarked on an intended route through the Straits of Gibraltar, on to Naples, through the Suez Canal stopping at Port Said and Aden, and later Colombo, before continuing to Australia. From Australia we were destined to take people to cruise in the Pacific, including places such as New Zealand, Fiji, and Hawaii, Vancouver in Canada, and San Francisco and Los Angeles in the United States.

During the five years I spent as a merchant seaman I left many ports in various craft. The smaller ships creep away rarely with anyone to witness their departure. Usually only the dock workers are present to cast off hawsers and quickly disappear to have their breakfasts. But the sailing of an ocean liner, especially an emigrant ship, was a complete contrast with much excitement and splendour.

When an emigrant ship sailed, it was quite a unique experience. The dockside was crowded with people waving, calling out and trying to catch the streamers thrown by the people on deck. These streamers eventually formed a multi-coloured network connecting the vessel with the shore, eventually to be broken as the vessel departed.

At the time of my first departure the people waving from the dockside fell into three categories. Those who were waving and laughing were the class of people who knew that those they were waving to were going on a fabulous holiday cruise from which they would return. The tearful ones were those waving goodbye to emigrants, whom they had sworn to visit one day but in reality recognised that it was unlikely that they would ever be able to afford to do so. The third type, were the family, loved ones, and brief alliances of crew members, saying goodbye for some twelve weeks.

Suddenly the faintest tremor came up from the bowels of the ship as the great power of her engines began to turn. The seagulls that wheeled overhead seemed to sense the change in the ship and began screeching their intention of accompanying the ship towards the mouth of the mighty Thames.

Lusty music blared over the ship's tannoys, — "Rule Britannia", "Life on the Ocean Wave", "Waltzing Matilda" and other stirring pieces. The captain gave the order to "cast off fore and aft". Then a lone bugle burst through with a fanfare, followed by deep-throated blasts of farewell from the ship's whistle, and the vessel began to move. This was the signal for increased calling from the shore, and more tears to flow from those anticipating a prolonged parting. As the ship slowly edged away from the quay the red ensign was raised and dramatically unfurled at the top of the ship's single mast. As the flag proudly whipped and cracked in the stiff breeze, some wag exclaimed, "Wow, what an erection!"

Two tugs pulled the *Orion* away from her berth through the limp, grey water, at the end of long

100

hawsers, whilst a third nudged her out into midstream with its bows pushing into her side like a piglet suckling at a sow. They pushed and pulled us out into the muddy Thames, and pointed us in the direction we were intended to go, towards the estuary under the ship's own power.

Across the widening gap between the ship and those who came to wave goodbye increasingly fervent calls of last contact floated on the air. The jollity of well-wishers calling to those leaving on a holiday of a lifetime was tempered by the tears of others. "If you don't like it there, tell them to "stuff it" and come straight back," yelled a Cockney from the quay. "Don't you worry, I will," a tremulous reply went back from an emigrant near where I was standing. If the truth were acknowledged it was difficult to imagine how the young family were to find the money to return to England without the government assistance that was sending them to Australia.

I also felt some trepidation about the journey I was embarking on. I was assured that I would return home, but three months away from home, and in a completely different environment, caused me considerable apprehension. However, I was determined that I would not reveal my worries to those I was to spend so much time and contact with, especially the worry of being seasick. One cabin mate put fears of this in my mind by warning me, "No throwing up in the cabin. If you feel seasick, get up on deck quick and throw up there."

Gradually the last streamer parted, the music ceased, and the frantically waving crowds faded into the distance. It was time to start the serious business of our voyage, although the tortuous route through grey limp waters of the River Thames to the mouth of the river, and past my home of Canvey Island, had still to be negotiated. My family were once again gathered on the sea wall, waving a table cloth so I could identify them. This time I was assured that I was truly "Australia bound".

As the *Orion* left the estuary of the Thames and the ship shuddered from the first significant waves to make her tremble slightly, passengers unaccustomed to shipboard life uttered excited cries. The more seasoned travellers assured them, "It'll be much worse in the Bay!" In due course this was found to be true.

The first lifeboat drill took place within hours of sailing. Passengers and crew were summoned to emergency stations and lifeboats by bells and klaxons, and blasts on the ship's siren. This was the signal to lock the dead lights over the portholes in our cabins and make our way to the upper decks. At first I prepared to go to my lifeboat station in a leisurely manner. Then I heard the ominous sliding of the watertight doors. Suddenly, horrified, I had visions of being trapped within a watertight compartment in the bowels of the ship and I dashed out of the cabin door. The watertight door outside my cabin was already tightly closed. In a state of panic I looked the other way. The door at the end of the passage was slowly moving to close. I shouted, "Wait", as if this would stop it, and charged along the passage and threw myself through the narrowing hole. I landed on the hard deck the other side. Quickly I clambered up and repeated the process at other places as I made my tortuous process to the upper decks via companionways which showed the way to reach the muster stations on the upper decks from the bowels of the ship.

Out on the open deck I felt less trapped and made my way to the appropriate muster station, where life jackets were handed round to passengers and crew. One full-breasted woman passenger asked me how to put the life jacket on and fasten it. I had no previous experience, but I was enjoying practising with her when a somewhat bumptious young officer began the official demonstration, thus bringing my fun to an end.

Before long we reached the westerly end of the English Channel. A coaster ship, much smaller than us, was bowing her way back along the route we had come. She seemed small and insignificant compared with our majestic floating hotel, and we sailed smoothly on whilst she bucketed fiercely in what to us was the relative calm of the Channel.

A small boat emerged from the mist of the indistinct shore and came towards us, a moustache of foam at its bow. The *Orion* slackened speed and wallowed sulkily as we prepared to send our pilot ashore in the minute pilot cutter that bounced along beside us awaiting his presence. We were now proceeding into deeper waters. Eventually the pilot clambered down the rope ladder and into the heaving pilot cutter alongside, and we began to navigate out into the Atlantic. The ship throbbed excitedly under my feet and the exhaust gases from the giant funnel above roared like some monstrous dragon into the sky.

Although we had been sailing for several hours, no one had told me what work I was to do. When I enquired of one of the other boy ratings what I was expected to do, he told me I was, "On anchor watch". Every two hours I was to take a mug of tea and a sandwich up to the man who was stationed in the bows of the ship.

At 10p.m. I duly collected a mug of tea and a sandwich and made my way to the bows of the ship. There, sure enough, was a man on watch by the big brass ship's bell. "I've brought you your tea and sandwich, sir", I explained. "Thanks a lot, son, and don't call me sir, Tom's the name", he replied. Later, at midnight, I repeated the journey whilst everyone had turned in for the night. The recipient looked pleased but puzzled by my service and asked me why I was doing it. When I explained he enlightened me that I had been the victim of a practical joke.

The next morning I found out that my first job was to be a bell-boy. This job involved sitting in full uniform near a signal board in a tiny cubicle, in the hot ship's galley. A bell would ring and an indicator would show, summoning me to an area where I was to collect a message and take it to other parts of the ship. The most frequent calls came from the radio office where I would collect telegrams that had been received by radio and deliver these to passengers.

The radio room was up near the bridge — a magical cavern! In there the air was full of the hiss of static with the occasional twitter of signals from some distant transmitter. I wondered how the radio officer could distinguish between the garbage I was hearing and yet suddenly recognise a call that was specifically for our ship; but then even I, as a newly appointed seaman, had quickly become attuned to the heartbeat of our ship. I could be asleep below and yet become wide awake and aware of a change of course or a variation in the throb of the engines. On talking to shipmates. I realised that I was far from alone in this affinity with the working of the ship. We were all of us, in some inexplicable way, tuned to the heartbeat pulse of the vessel.

The job of bellboy had its moments of excitement and was the source of spicy tales to relate to other boy ratings. Although those of us who carried out this duty sometimes embellished our tales there were occasions when the truth was interesting enough. Such as the time when I delivered a telegram to two scantily dressed girls who tried to encourage me to spend a little time in their cabin, but in my young innocence I declined in fear of getting into trouble.

Another young lad on bell duty was to cause a major stir later in the voyage, when we were in the Mediterranean. This boy had been the target of teasing by one of the adult crew members, and he was quite miserable about it. One day he found himself alone in the radio office. He took a blank radio message form and wrote on it, "*Congratulations Son, you've won £75,000 on the pools. Dad.*"

The message was delivered to the tormentor, who promptly told his superior officer where he could stick

105

his job and arranged transfer from crew's quarters to a first-class cabin.

Once the boy rating realised the enormity of his crime he promptly disappeared, leaving a note that implied he was "going over the side". The ship was turned round and retraced her recent Mediterranean route with searchlights probing the darkness. Crew and passengers alike scanned the ship's bubbling wake hoping to catch sight of him. It was a few hours before the bell-boy was found hiding in the crew's toilets. In due course the boy was fined three day's pay, not that this was particularly great, considering our meagre pay as boy-ratings.

The *Orion*, being an elderly ship, had no stabilisers. As she left home waters and turned south round Ushant, the force of the Atlantic waves made themselves felt, and many passengers stayed in their cabins, trying to hide from the severe weather that held the ship in its grip and took the swagger out of the most seasoned travellers. The wind blew hard, the spray flew, and *Orion* now raised her bows high into the air. She seemed to hang poised and then plunged sideways as she corkscrewed over the sea. Now I fully understood the reason for the little ledges (fiddles) around the edges of the tables. Even so there was much broken crockery.

I was worried that I might embarrass myself and succumb to sea sickness, but fortunately this did not happen. I actually felt exhilarated by the battering the ship was taking, and I had full confidence in her strength and the ability of her officers. To me I felt excited in the way I had enjoyed the thrill of a roller coaster at the fairground as a youngster. In my bunk at night I found the rising and falling movement very soothing and quickly fell asleep.

One day the Chief Steward asked me, "Do you sing?" I said that I was once a church choir boy, but omitted to mention that since my voice had broken it sounded like a creaking door. But the promise of 2s each Sunday, on top of the meagre pay of £9 a month, was enough to encourage me to sing at the Sunday service for first-class passengers.

On the next Sunday at sea I duly reported to the first-class lounge on the upper deck (closer to God) to participate in the service for the passengers. The crew "choir" assembled together in best uniform in front of the passenger audience. Being wary of putting off my neighbours with my ghastly voice I sang in an undertone. But it didn't take me long to realise that those either side of me were also there under false pretences.

As we left later, the seaman who had been singing flat throughout said to me, "It was really good to sing with someone with a good voice". The other one who had been out of tune throughout said, "That's the best I've ever sung, so it must be your influence". I thought that I could justifiably accept this little extra income.

Later in the voyage my position as a member of the ship's choir caused me to attend a burial at sea where we were required to sing a hymn or two. A member of the crew died and he had made it clear that he wished to be buried at sea. At the time of the committal a collection of the crew, including the choir, were assembled on the after deck. The ship was hove to and the Captain conducted a short service. Then the canvas bag enclosed body was slid down a kind of slide from beneath a Union Jack. Duly weighted, the bag took a gracious dive below the waves and the ship continued on its way. At the next port mail arrived for the deceased from HM Tax Inspector. On the envelope were the words "Please Forward." I thought this was going to prove difficult!

In due course we reached Gibraltar. The wind dropped and the Mediterranean sun shone in all its splendour. The voyage suddenly took on a true holiday spirit. The passengers emerged from their self-imposed seclusion and excitedly queued to go ashore to explore the Rock. It was a lively evening for the crew also. The bars were full of sailors, and the streets thronged with them later as they wandered back to the ship in good humour.

We left Gibraltar after only a short stay to continue on the next leg of our voyage, towards Naples in Italy. This would take about three days. The Mediterranean is a much more civilised sea than the Atlantic Ocean that had dominated the Bay of Biscay on the voyage down to Gibraltar. Now the passengers felt confident to walk the decks and bask in the sunshine.

Not long after we left Gibraltar I was sitting in the crew cabin with a seasoned seaman. "Do you feel that, son?" he asked. "Feel that vibration? We're really increasing speed now. You watch the old *Orion* shift now. We must be doing twenty-six knots already, may be even her top whack of twenty-eight." You could sense his feeling of pride in the old liner.

For some reason I sensed we were near land as soon as I woke on the morning we were due to arrive at Naples. It was before six in the morning but I was instantly awake. I dressed and left the cabin quietly, so as to not disturb my cabin mates and scampered up to the well deck. I was out on deck completely alone and watched the first streaks of reddish-coloured daylight exploring over the distant horizon. The shore came closer quicker than I expected. The curve of the bay of Naples was still distantly blurred, so I could, initially, only form an impression of the brightness of it with the white buildings around it.

As we came close to the Bay of Naples, passing between Capri and Sorrento, I imagined that we must look enormously majestic in comparison to the multitude of yachts with white sails that scudded around us. It was now possible to see the buildings more clearly. They seemed to be made of a hotch-potch of terraces that appeared to tumble down to the sea. The vivid blue sea lapped at the feet of the buildings, and above was a cloudless sky.

Soon the *Orion* edged into the port of Naples. It welcomed visitors with open arms, and sometimes more for the sex-starved crew, but not for a poor financially-strapped boy rating such as me. I went ashore with another boy rating. We wore the almost universal daytime dress of seamen off-duty of a white T-shirt and jeans — plus, of course, an inevitable leather belt with a fancy buckle.

It was in the port of Naples I learned the usefulness of the seamen's missions. These are run by religious groups for the benefit of poor distressed seamen. They are found in ports around the world and they are the place to go if you don't have any money, which as a boy rating I had little. We used them to hunt down local girls, but there was a penalty involved.

The missions would put on dance nights which brought together randy seamen and local maidens, presumably of religious persuasion. The evenings would start innocently enough with modern music played on a simple record player. We would use this time to assess which girls were likely to "respond favourably" and we would lavish attention on them. This cost very little because no alcohol was on sale, and to treat them to half-time tea and biscuits was nothing to a seamen, not even a poor boy rating.

The "in" dance at that time was the "creep". This was a close dance, where the man planted their hands low on their partner's buttocks and shuffled around the floor, with dancing the furthest thing from their mind. The beauty about the creep was that you didn't need to know how to dance. All that was required was to be able to shuffle around, and hang onto buttocks. All of which was good for my puberty with the sap rising, but perhaps not so good for my morality, although most of it was all in the mind!

The true cost of the evening's entertainment came after the half-time tea break, when we were required to visit a chapel and sing a couple of hymns and participate in prayers, thus delaying our amorous intentions. But if our selection of girls had been accurate the chapel session did not prevent some girls from proving willing partners later in the evening, although this was often the subject of exaggeration by the seamen, especially destitute boy ratings.

All too soon it was time to depart from Naples on the next stage of our voyage. Our route was heading for the Suez Canal, at the eastern end of the Mediterranean. But just hours before we were due to enter the Canal news came of the outbreak of conflict there. The ship was darkened down, dead lights were clamped over the portholes, and a new course was set for Malta. A revised itinerary was announced which was to take us back through the Mediterranean, out of the Straits of Gibraltar, down the coast of Africa and round the Cape of Good Hope. News of the Suez conflict was the cause of much excitement among the crew members and it provoked stories of the Second World War from the older seamen, although it was the cause of much concern to our families back home. For me it was pure excitement.

There was a buzz of excitement in spite of the possible danger, and some seasoned seamen exploited this to the full. Whilst I was on deck gazing at the layer of bow wash created by our increase in speed, one old tar said to me, "You're in a war zone now lad. You can watch for dolphins, but you are better to look out for torpedoes. If you miss a dolphin you'll see another one day. But torpedoes? . . . They're different! You only get one chance to see them."

111

I was alarmed of course, but it was only later that I realised the whole purpose of the conversation was to wind me up. It certainly had that affect for a short while, but exhilaration quickly replaced the alarm.

To make up for the sudden change of sailing route, passengers were served free champagne, although in reality they were quite excited by the drama that was unfolding. Most of the crew were equally excited, and this was enhanced by the provision of free beer. During this time, at my station in the galley, the indicator bells began ringing like a pin-table as passengers summoned the bell-boy to send telegrams to loved ones to inform them of the change of plans. In the wireless room the equipment rattled and chattered as the radio officers worked like stink to deal with the mass of messages going out and coming in.

CHAPTER
FIVE

INDECENT EXPOSURE

Following the brief unscheduled stopover in Malta, we embarked on the announced revised route to Australia — back through the Straits of Gibraltar and on to Cape Town in South Africa with a stop at the Canary Islands on the way. For three more days we sailed back towards the Straits of Gibraltar. The clouds were low and thick but this did little to quell the excitement of the crew caused by the news of the Suez events. For me, on my first voyage, of course, it mattered little which route we took. Every port was to be a completely new experience for me.

As we passed back through the Straits of Gibraltar one veteran sailor said to me, "Well son, you are saying goodbye to the sunny Mediterranean. It's out into the wild Atlantic for us. You'll notice the difference." Considering the battering we had gone through earlier in the trip while crossing the Bay of Biscay I couldn't imagine what we faced could be much worse. And, after all, the *Orion* was a very big ship, almost an island as far as I was concerned.

Once out of the Mediterranean the sea was distinctly different, and reflected to some extent the kind of

113

buffeting we had experienced in the Bay of Biscay earlier in the voyage. But now the sea appeared more benevolent. We sailed down through the ocean, on green white-topped rollers like moving hills. Yet the sun still shone a warm welcome, and as the ship's bows sliced through the water with her increased speed, we were joined by a school of porpoises which plunged and surfaced in their play. The blue grey bodies dived in succession with effortless precision to reappear minutes later still in exact formation ahead of the wake of the bow. Passengers and crew alike crowded for positions at the ship's rails to watch the porpoises, shouting with excitement and delight.

As we pushed further south, the sea turned aquamarine under the azure sky and the trade winds wafted gently into the rush of the ship as she proceeded along her new route. The first port of call when we left the Mediterranean was the sun bleached port of Las Palmas in the Canary Islands, where we were to spend just a few hours before heading south down the coast of West Africa.

As we approached the port one of the older seamen said to me, "Have you had a woman yet?" I had to admit that at fifteen years of age sex had not featured in my life. "Here's ten bob, go ashore and have one on me", was the generous offer. This was accompanied by tips on how to spot a brothel and what to do inside. In spite of this benevolent gesture I went ashore full of trepidation. I was going into new territory!

I wandered up and down side streets of whitewashed cottages but found no places with red lights outside, or girls loitering in the doorways. Fortunately, on a second passing up a particular street, a door opened, and an elderly woman beckoned me inside. I was apprehensive that she might expect me to go with her. However, when we got inside she summoned a collection of pretty girls for me to choose from. I chose one who seemed the closest I could get to my tender age.

The girl took me to a room that contained a double bed and a sink in one corner. One wall consisted of see-through partitioning blocks through which people could see and hear everything going on. I found this most disconcerting.

The girl asked me for 15s but I showed her I only had ten and she was satisfied with this. My first experience of sex was brief and far from memorable for me and I am sure even less so for my brief companion, but I found myself thinking about the girl all the way back to the ship. "Why did someone so young and pretty have to make a living in that way? Wouldn't it be wonderful to turn up one day and offer to take her home with me?"

When I got back to the ship my benefactor wanted to be assured I had "lost my cherry". "I'll bet you thought she was beautiful, and wished you could take her away from that life". I was amazed that someone could so accurately recognise what I felt. But I was, of course, just reflecting what he had probably experienced as a youngster. However, this attitude towards the girl stayed with me for some time after this brief initial experience.

We left the Canary Islands and sailed into the South Atlantic bound for Cape Town. We headed south and, in due course, crossed the Equator which involved the customary initiation of those crossing "the line" for the first time. For the passengers there was an elaborate and dignified ceremony with much dressing up, and the presentation of a certificate ostensibly signed by no less than King Neptune himself.

Making the first crossing of the Equator was far from dignified for crew members. A list was formed of those who were crossing the line for the first time. In effect this list could only be formed from subtle questioning ahead of the event, because no official list existed. So, spies began investigations for likely candidates well ahead of reaching equatorial waters.

On the afternoon of the day of the crossing of the Equator, the unfortunate victims to meet King Neptune were hunted down, stripped naked and brought to the well deck to meet His Majesty under the blazing sun to provide amusement for the assembled crew.

The sight that welcomed the candidates waiting to receive the honour of entering the King's realm was theatrically organised. King Neptune sat on his throne with his wife and courtiers on either side of him.

King Neptune was in fact the grizzly bosun, suitably adorned with a golden crown, reminiscent of a leftover from Christmas, a blonde beard and flowing wig constructed from ship's rope carefully teased apart. He wore a striped toga and held a trident, with one prong strangely pointing in a completely different direction to the other two.

The King's wife, in spite of efforts to make the bosun's mate give some impression of femininity, was clearly someone you wouldn't want to meet on a dark night. The King's assembled courtiers were a motley crew, rigged in a wild assortment of coloured rags with a most strange collection of items, including swollen condoms filled with a variety of coloured suspicious-looking liquids.

Neptune, in his regal position on his throne, drew attentive silence with the waving of his injured trident. One of his courtiers greeted the august visitor, bowing low before him with a flourish and saying, "We welcome you, Your Majesty, to this humble ship and we hope you will allow these (pointing to the naked gathering of candidates) unworthy creatures to enter your illustrious realm. Kindly accept a glass of Ocean Nectar", with which the King was handed a generously filled glass of rum.

After draining the glass in one gulp, the King addressed the assembly in a suitably ocean deep, gravely voice, "What ship?"

"*Orion*", replied another courtier.

"To where are you bound?" demanded King Neptune.

"To Australia, the land of the kangaroo and the magic boomerang," answered yet another well-rehearsed courtier, while the King's wife displayed horror at such a place to visit, while adjusting her breast as one soup plate was drooping.

"Now dear, we mustn't be late for the mermaid's ball," she wailed in a falsetto voice that sounded rather like a creaky door.

"An indomitable place to visit," the King thundered, "But that's your business if you are determined to visit heathens. Avast, bring forth the candidates," said King Neptune, downing another glass of Ocean Nectar.

Flogged forward by a heavily tattooed crew member wearing a grass skirt and wielding a whip fashioned from a tarred rope teased loose, the unfortunates were forced to parade their nakedness around the well deck and line up in front of King Neptune.

"Are these scrawny mortals worthy of entry to my kingdom?" Neptune demanded.

"Unworthy they surely are, Your Majesty," whined Miss Whiplash, "But they humbly beseech King Neptune to inflict penalties upon them to make them worthy of your realm, oh Majesty."

"In that case, proceed to prove their worth," instructed the by now half-sloshed King.

The range of indignities then heaped upon us cannot surely be relayed without attracting the pity of the reader. Every time I tried to answer questions put to me, a brush covered in vividly red soft soap was rammed in my mouth, and if I didn't attempt to reply to a question, the brush was poked in my rear end.

I was fortunately too young to shave, so I could not suffer the fate of a mature seaman who had half of his beard shaved off, and when he yelled in painful protest, he suffered the discomfort of having his mouth filled with a vile concoction. But my humiliation was just as thorough in being covered from head to foot in a foul-smelling, suspiciously coloured jelly-like substance that subsequently took numerous showers and several days to remove.

The jollity increased as the Ocean Nectar flowed freely among all the assembled participants, and even the victims, to encourage them to "cooperate". Buckets of water were brought into play and eventually all within the vicinity were soaked, and the well deck was awash with water and slime. Now, perhaps not surprisingly, even His Majesty was looking the worse for wear.

But, in due course, the ordeal was over. The fire hoses were turned on us, the bruising power of which knocked the wind out of us, but cleaned much of the "gunge" from our bodies, and we were allowed to escape to the showers to restore our dignity, although it was many days before the "scent" of King Neptune's party disappeared completely. In due course, I received a certificate declaring I had crossed the line, and been admitted to the realm of King Neptune. Needless to say, this certificate was kept safely to ensure I would not be submitted to such indignity again.

As we pushed even further southwards, below decks it became hot and uncomfortable for sleeping in a ship built with no air conditioning for crew. Metal scoops could, in fair weather, be pushed out of portholes to direct a flow of tropical air into the cabin from the ship's movement. But this was of limited use in a cabin with twelve crew and some crew members took to sleeping out on deck under the night stars. I did

119

attempt this on one occasion, but a sudden squall left me soaked with rain and I never attempted it again.

A few days off from our scheduled arrival at the port of Cape Town, near the Cape of Good Hope, down at the southern tip of Africa, there was an obvious change in the movement of the ship. It no longer pitched or rolled as previously. The new movement seemed a combination of the two. The "Cape Rollers" caused a kind of corkscrew movement, rolling and pitching at the same time (the most sickening of movements), and this sparked off a painful feeling in my stomach.

Having never been seasick before I assumed that I was now going to be embarrassed by this inadequacy and told no one what I was suffering. I dreaded being shamed by seasickness which was the cause of so much amusement to seasoned seamen. Then I collapsed on duty. The ship's doctor was called and he immediately diagnosed acute appendicitis.

I was taken to the ship's sick bay where the doctor told me they were increasing speed to try and get to Cape Town so that I could be operated on ashore. However, if necessary he would carry out the operation himself and was consulting advisers ashore by radio. In passing he asked how old I was and expressed disbelief when I said I was fifteen years of age. "You must be wrong lad," he said, "You cannot become a seaman below the age of sixteen." Now the truth was out and I explained the mathematical error that was made during my enlistment. So, my parents had to be contacted to be put in the picture regarding my situation, resulting in deep concern at home on Canvey Island.

While lying in the bed in the sick bay, in much pain, and sweating in the tropical conditions, the hospital orderly took the opportunity to encourage me to recover.

The orderly was an obnoxious, alcoholic "Scouse" with no compassion. It transpired that he had been told that his shore leave in Cape Town had been cancelled in order to care for me. As this was his first visit to Cape Town this did not endear me to him. He told me horrific stories of what medical intricacies were being planned for the removal of my appendix, unless I made a remarkable recovery. It worked, the pains subsided and I was back on duty before we reached Cape Town. I still have my appendix today.

In Cape Town I headed straight for the central park. I proceeded to chat up every young girl I could. All of the girls were black, the newness of which only added to my enthusiasm, as there were very few black people in my home area. Another crew member saw my actions and warned me that it was against the law to mix with other races in South Africa. This was my first experience of apartheid. It stunned me and it is something that I have never been able to come to terms with. Since that time I have had many good friends of other nationalities and without exception they have all enriched my life.

We left Cape Town and turned into the Indian Ocean heading onwards towards Australia. It was in this ocean that I saw my first albatross. I have seen many sea birds on my travels, but none as awesome as the albatross. They are wonderful great birds. Some old tars told me that harm to one of these birds would result in bad luck for all those connected with the perpetrator.

In due course we sailed into Australian waters, gradually putting people ashore as we sailed around the coast. As we approached Sydney on our route from Melbourne we passed Botany Bay. The ship's daily news sheet made romantic reading of this and its association with Captain Cook's explorations, but, as I recall, Captain Cook reported rather disparagingly about it. Furthermore, Captain Cook apparently initially bypassed what is now called Sydney Harbour, although he named it Port Jackson, as he failed to appreciate its worth. However, it is easy to see how Cook had failed to recognise the value of Port Jackson. You don't realise the full splendour of one of the most spectacular harbours in the world until you pass the headlands that flank its mouth, obscuring the wonder that lies within.

We finally berthed at Sydney where we were due to stay for an extended period before going on a Pacific cruise. As we slowly edged into our berth, the ship's public address system blasted out Australia's best-known song, "Waltzing Matilda" which eulogises a sheep rustler. In Sydney we joined our sister-ship the *Oronsay* on which I should have originally sailed. This gave me the opportunity to meet again friends who should have been my shipmates.

It was during our extended stay in dock in Sydney that some bright junior officer came up with the magic idea that it would be useful to practice abandoning ship. His idea was to lower several of the lifeboats on the seaward side of the ship, and create a rowing race between the three departments of the ship — the deckhands, the catering staff and the engineering attendants. Big mistake!

As expected, as soon as the deckhands' boat touched the water, they rapidly rowed away like ferrets out of the bag in an impressive display of coordinated precision movement, whilst the engine room men were piddling around in panic-stricken circles. The catering staff in the meantime couldn't even manage to detach their boats from the davits. Our pathetic attempts at self-survival became a complete farce and embarrassment. The officer responsible for the whole fiasco was further alarmed when it appeared that media photographers were in action from the quay, and the exercise was quickly abandoned. Needless to say, the exercise was not attempted again.

Near the docks in Sydney Harbour was a hamburger bar which many ships' crew members frequented on the way back from the local bars. It was in a very seedy area of the docks and we were all familiar with Margo, who was a short-term companion who provided horizontal refreshment for anyone who could afford her prices.

While in the hamburger bar late one evening I wanted to go to the toilet that was out in the back yard. When I got out there I interrupted Margo carrying out her business with someone who could afford her prices. In this case, she was providing vertical refreshment for her customer. I retraced my way back through the hamburger bar and went around the side of the

123

building to pee up against the wall in a darkened back alley. Whilst in full flow I was suddenly illuminated by a bright searchlight from a police wagon.

Two burly policemen grabbed hold of me and bundled me roughly into the back of the police wagon with an assortment of drunks. Fortunately, my departure was witnessed by some crew members, and the word soon got around that "one of the boys was in trouble".

At the police station I was finger-printed and made to walk a white line that proved I wasn't drunk. I thought that this would be good news that would result in my immediate release. But it resulted in a more serious charge of indecent exposure. I did wonder how one could "expose" in a pitch black back alley. However, I found myself at the tender age of fifteen years in a large cell with a load of drunks. In the middle of the cell was a toilet with no seat or privacy, and my bed was a hard bench and a disgusting blanket.

A few hours later I was bailed out by the prostitute whose business I had interrupted. When I tried to thank her, she only treated me to a stream of profanities. Within a couple of days two plain clothes policemen came and collected me from the ship and took me to appear in court. This seemed a rather over the top exercise for a minor offence by a fifteen year old. The judge listened sympathetically to my explanation of the reason for having to pee up the wall, but still fined me £12, which was a considerable lump out of my salary.

Our Pacific cruise was a contrast to the voyage out to Australia. Gone were the emigrants and the vessel became a giant holiday home. All the passengers seemed wealthy to me, and hell bent on enjoying themselves. The cruise took in visits to New Zealand, Fiji, Hawaii, Canada and San Francisco and Los Angeles in the United States.

Not long into the Pacific cruise, a couple taking a "one off" holiday began to show a particular interest in me. The wife was an intriguing woman with a strange croaky voice. Her husband said that she was an animal lover. He said she had a mink in her wardrobe, a jaguar in the garage, and a frog in her throat. I wondered if she also had an ass to pay for it all!

This couple clearly seemed to have taken a shine to me and singled me out to talk to when I was on duty. They expressed surprise that someone so young would choose the life of a seaman, foregoing the comfort of family life. For some perverse reason I told them I was an orphan, and my life at sea was providing me with the home and companionship I needed.

It was a pathetic and wicked thing to say, but once uttered, I felt committed to the lie. The woman's eyes filled with tears. She explained that they couldn't have children, and they owned a "station out back". I would be welcome to go there and stay for as long as I wished.

I found myself wondering how people made a living out of a railway station. All the stations at home were owned by the government, and they were losing money. It took a more seasoned seaman to explain that, in Australia, the word "station" referred to a farm. With this explanation I assumed that perhaps the term had its origins in that, as the farms in Australia were so isolated, they provided a welcome resting place for travellers.

Although I genuinely liked the young couple with the sprawling farm, I couldn't imagine living out in the back of beyond. In any case I did have a large extended family in Essex to go home to. I was relieved when the couple left the cruise at Los Angeles to fly home, and I could push the shameful deceit into the back of my mind.

While in Los Angeles, one afternoon I went to a cinema that showed strip shows. I was still just fifteen years of age and the age limit for entry was eighteen. I didn't look fifteen, let alone eighteen, but with the bravado of youth I went along, paid my money, and was admitted to a cinema with a mere scattering of men and a lone woman spectator. I did wonder why a woman would go into such a place. Perhaps she recruited men — for some reason?

A beam of light shot onto the screen and the audience could be felt to suddenly become attentive, apart from the lone woman who was looking everywhere but at the screen. On the screen appeared a girl in the early stages of undress. She was still wearing a bra and petticoat, which she hitched up with one hand to reveal a stocking secured by a suspender. A man nearby began wheezing. There were mutterings of "be quiet", but there were no words to be heard from the film, just the music — supposedly erotic.

The girl on the screen slowly proceeded through the routine of undressing with some resemblance of being in time to the music. The bra was gradually peeled back to reveal first one over-generous breast and then the other. After some gyrations the girl disrobed until she was swaying in a g-string with not so much as a pubic hair in sight. It was not what I had imagined and even in my state of innocence seemed boring. The sense of disappointment was not relieved by subsequent short films, all of which seemed to be re-enacting the same routine as the first.

I left the cinema before the end of the screening and spent the rest of my money on some books that I hoped would prove more erotic than the films. I walked back to the ship because I had no money left for a taxi. On the way back I was picked up by two friendly policemen in a patrol car. I hid the books in my shirt because I was worried that I might get into trouble for having been in the cinema whilst underage. But my worries were unfounded and they kindly took me right to the foot of the first-class gangway, much to the interest of many onlookers.

Later in the voyage we visited Vancouver and as its skyline hove into view one could not avoid being awed by its spectacular backdrop of dramatic snow-capped mountains. I was fortunate that a departing passenger offered to take me on a tour of the area. She turned up to the ship in a chauffeur-driven stretched limo and whisked me away from the first class gangway, much to the envy of the other boy ratings. This was a just reward for someone as polite and crawly as I was.

As part of the Pacific cruise we visited Fiji. Together with two other crew members I was taken into a tiny village in the hills where I was fascinated, as young boys would be, to find all the women bare breasted. While in this village I first experienced a drink of kava, a mildly intoxicating drink made from pepper root. I didn't find the taste at all interesting, and I was even less impressed when I was told how it was made. It seems that kava is traditionally prepared by chewing the plant into a pulp before spitting the resulting mess into bowls and adding water, after which it ferments.

I later found out that although kava was originally prepared in this way, now, to meet the requirements of modern tourists, the kava is ground in a more hygienic way during preparation. But the result remains the same. It looked like dishwater, and tasted much like it also. I had read from stories of Captain Cook's travels that kava juice has a stupefying drug-like effect, but all I noticed was a mild numbing of my tongue. My first and last drink of kava was from a coconut shell in deference to tourist expectations. It did not impress me at all.

It was unofficially estimated that half of the crew of the *Orion* were "queer". At that time, homosexuality was a subject of grave taboo, and largely secretive in shore life, and until then I had never even considered such things. The extent of my knowledge was that some lads were "pansies". To me that meant a bit soft — nothing to do with sexuality. I had no knowledge or understanding of homosexuality, even though my father had at one time tried to explain it to me before I went away to sea. Here, on the happy ship *Orion*, homosexuality was rife and accepted as another facet of life. It was blatantly displayed in this part of the

Merchant Navy, even to the extent that some of the "queers" actually carried handbags and other feminine items, even when working in passenger quarters.

The "queers" were particularly evident in the catering staff. Few were deck hands that I recall, probably because the work was recognised as too masculine, although I do remember one who worked in the engine room whose huge build was far from effeminate. While a novice boy rating I was standing in a corridor talking to a more experienced boy in my cabin when this burly engineer walked by. The boy with me whistled and blew him a kiss. I waited for the anticipated clip round the ear, but all the burly recipient did was to blow a kiss back. He was as bent, as they used to say, as a £9 note. In my naivety I was astounded. But in time I came to learn that "gender-bending" was just a part of life of which I was ignorant.

Many of these men were excellent cabin staff and waiters who took extreme pride in the way that they carried out their duties. I assume that this was because they found the domesticity of the work appealing to their "gender-bender". They were generous and open people whom I always found willing to help when needed, without obligation. Having made it quite clear I was not interested in homosexual behaviour, I was never propositioned by any of them and I found them interesting people to talk to.

Being young and curious about their homosexuality, I quizzed one of them, who was about as camp as a row of tents, about it. "She" was very open and easy to talk

129

to and explained it in this way. "I remember one day being out on a school trip in a park. We boys were chasing the girls around and it didn't feel right to me. So I started chasing the boys instead, and this felt right. I've been doing it right ever since".

As part of the crew entertainment "Sods Operas" were organised periodically. This was a time when those with talent would put on a show in the crew bar. The "queers" would put on "full drag", with glamorous gowns and make up and many of them were the star performers. We would all gather in the bar with a few pints of the cheap beer available and sit back and enjoy the show.

There were many fine acts in the "Sod's Operas", but my favourite was a pantry man called Charlie. He had a deep resonant voice. He was superb. His rendering of "Granada" was as good as any professional singer. There was a fellow who imitated Mario Lanza and Joseph Locke, who were popular singers at the time. And there were two brothers who mimed to records and caused great hilarity when the larger of the two appeared to be singing in the high-pitched voice of a girl.

One seaman, from Southend, was able to imitate the voice of a very young child. He dressed up as a little girl and was "interviewed" by another crew member. During the interview the little girl came out with a torrent of obscenities and double-talk in her childlike voice, which had the audience doubled up with laughter.

130

On one occasion a cleaned up version of a "Sods Opera" was put on in port to entertain the passengers. In addition to the crew entertainers, a shore-based magician was brought on board. The highlight of his act was to move a collection of caps about on a table. The passengers were required to identify where baby chicks were hidden under the caps. Unbeknown to the visiting magician, some of the crew had been feeding the chicks brandy. When, at the finale of his act, he lifted the caps to reveal all, the chicks were found to be legless, much to the mirth of the crew members and the bewilderment of the magician.

Another form of entertainment for both crew and passengers was to hold boxing tournaments. Contestants were paid the princely sum of 30s to fight — a considerable sum for youngsters on my lowly pay. I also thought a spot of boxing would help to dispel my baby-like appearance, and demonstrate my masculinity.

I had made friends with two older seamen, both of who had extensive boxing experience. They decided to train me for a forthcoming crew competition for the entertainment of the passengers. These two benevolent souls consisted of a six foot plus former Golden Gloves champion and an eighteen stone hooligan who terrorised the rest of the crew.

The guy who was a former golden gloves champion was tall and good looking, and moved lightly on his feet, in spite of being in the heavyweight category. This partly explained why he was a former golden gloves champion, and had remained good looking. When sparring with him his punches stung and were delivered

131

snappily, and he quickly moved out of reach before I could strike back.

My other trainer was slow, heavy and ponderous, and very ugly! His face resembled a mixture of that of a gorilla mixed with that of a pig. It was obvious that both of his ears had been bitten off at some time, thoroughly chewed and stuck back on his head with no consideration for appearance. Surely one of them had been put back upside down? He had a big, cropped, skull and a flattened fighter's nose. The nose spread out below the rough slab of his forehead and overhanging scarred eyebrows. His face appeared to have been hacked by various instruments that had left an intricate array of scars. Perhaps the one concession Mr Ponderous' gorilla features made to his human origins was his follicularly-challenged scalp, but which was also disfigured by scars that resembled the backside of a walrus. But I'm sure his mother loved him!

Whilst "Mr Golden Gloves" punched with sharp painful jabs and danced out of reach, he hit me with just enough power to teach me without destroying me. Mr Ponderous just stood in front of me and soaked up my hardest punches with no recognition of the devastation I was trying to inflict. Then he would hit back with a slow ponderous swing that I could see coming, but felt rooted to the floor and unable to get away. Wherever such blows landed it felt as if the whole of my body shuddered. I am sure that the blows Mr Ponderous delivered contributed considerably to the subsequent deterioration in my hearing resulting from his determination to reshape my ears to match his own.

132

Each afternoon I was summoned to appear on the well deck in searing heat to skip and attack a punch ball that weighed far more than I did. At fifteen years of age I was a five-foot-six, seven-stone weed, and herein lay a major problem. There was no crew member small enough to match me and, consequently, it was obvious that I was destined to fight opponents much bigger than myself.

Being aware of my weight predicament, my worthy trainers proceeded on a strategy to fatten me up. I embarked on a high protein, weight increasing diet, which included raw eggs, full cream milk, and steaks, courtesy of Mr Ponderous via the first-class passengers' galley. All to no avail — not a pound went on my weight.

The day before my big fight I thought I would look more impressive if I entered the ring with a nice sun tan. But I overdid it and ended up looking like a walking beetroot. Eventually I passed out with sunstroke. It was clear I couldn't possibly fight, much to the disgust of my trainers. Far from being sympathetic to my condition, they made it clear that they thought that I had deliberately tried to avoid my fight.

On a later occasion I was due to fight another seaman who was the closest to my weight, although considerably older. I felt quite happy at the prospect of this match. He was a good looking chap with perfect teeth, and I reasoned that perhaps his good looks indicated that he was not very experienced. He could

133

not be worse to face than Mr Ponderous on the well deck in searing heat.

On the night of my bout I faced Mr Good Looking across the ring. But he looked very different. He clearly had false teeth and once these had been removed his features were transformed. He no longer looked handsome but now appeared quite ferocious. What followed was three rounds of humiliation for me that I was lucky to survive, probably because my opponent spent most of the time holding me up.

The overhead lights splashed a lagoon of brightness over the ring as my opponent and I prepared for the fight. My stomach was tied up in knots and I felt sick with fear. I could feel nerves in my upper legs twitching and hoped that this was not visible to the onlookers, and I hoped I wouldn't vacate my bowels.

The bell went for round one and we circled each other like predators; he flicked out a left hand that I feinted and it missed my head and struck my shoulder, supposedly harmless, but it really hurt. Another flurry of jabs and then a right cross that caught me full in the face. I tasted blood, and unfortunately, it was mine; my nose was damaged and bleeding, I had no defence against the crippling punches he was throwing. I think it was Sir Richard Grenville who famously said, "We have not yet begun to fight!" Well that was very true in my case. Blessedly the bell went and I returned to my corner a fumbling wreck after only three minutes of combat.

I sat on my stool and tried to pay attention to the instructions my trainers were giving me, and not take too much notice of their scolding of the mistakes I had committed. All too soon the bell rang and it was time to go out again into that harsh pool of light.

The second round was much the same as that dished out in the first round. It was a one-sided assault, with me trying to avoid getting hurt too badly, but not seriously hitting back in case I angered my opponent further. I was conscious of the fact that the onlookers were screaming at me to strike back but my gloves felt like lumps of lead, and my legs failed to respond to my brain's instructions to get moving.

Then a right cross hit me above my eye and I knew I was bleeding in another place. I was ready to lie down, but the bell rang and took the opportunity away from me. As I shambled back to my corner I looked enough like the missing link to give Darwin food for thought.

The only official, the referee, came over to my corner and peered at my injuries. Surely he must stop the punishment? But, no, I must go out again. Suddenly, as I sat there listening to the innate instructions from my frustrated corner-men, a calmness came over me, that was also to help me in my later life. It was the calmness of fatalism — what will be, will be.

I came out for the third and final round a different person. I still got hit, and it still hurt. But now I hit back, not in anger but with a newfound calmness. I struck some good blows and the fight was no longer one-sided. The final outcome was beyond doubt, the other guy won overwhelmingly. But I had salvaged considerable self-esteem. Even more importantly, I had come to the conclusion that boxing was not the way for me to prove my masculinity, and it was certainly not worth the 30s I was paid to entertain the crew.

The opportunities for fun seemed unending on the happy-go-lucky *Orion*, and neither the officers, nor the passengers, seemed offended by our antics. But one prank got out of hand. It started below decks when some of the crew brought water pistols back from a shore visit. Pistol fights between waiters extended into the dining salons and it was barely tolerable for a first-class waiter to be "shot" whilst ladling soup. But the final straw came when one waiter passed through the rotating doors between the dining room and the galley, only to be knocked back through them by the full blast of the galley fire hose. Water fights were banned, but still a few die-hards carried out "shoot-outs" in the saloons with pointed forefinger and "cocked" thumb, with the victims collapsing in the middle of serving meals. The passengers accepted all of this with good humour.

Following my first trip to sea on the *Orion*, I spent almost two years sailing with her. Subsequently I served on several other liners, including my first intended vessel, the *Oronsay*. On one such trip, whilst I was still a boy rating, three of us had a special job called "pantry boys". It had nothing to do with pantries but really involved doing all sorts of special cleaning jobs. We had our own uniform which consisted of blue and white close-striped blouse-style jackets, which we wore over white T-shirts and black trousers and shoes. Our personal touch to the uniform was to substitute heavy chrome lavatory chains for belts. These uniforms were quite distinct from other crew members and this was to prove to be to our disadvantage.

One of the advantages of this job was that our work was carried out in the luxury of the first class passenger areas, and this enabled two of us to become friendly with two American girls who were cruising with their parents.

It was forbidden for crew members to be unofficially in passenger areas, especially at night. We arranged to meet these two girls in the darkened children's play area on the top deck in the middle of one clear starlit night. I took my girl into the Wendy House, but it turned out to be too small and uncomfortable to be seriously amorous.

The girls suggested we should go to their cabin, which was next to that of their parents. This was too tempting an opportunity to pass up, but there were night watchmen on the inside corridors and we had to avoid them. Fortunately, the girls were in an expensive cabin adjacent to an outside deck. So we arranged for them to go to their cabin and open the porthole to enable us to scramble in.

As we were in the process of getting in through the porthole their mother looked out and saw us and began screaming blue murder. We legged it away as fast as we could and escaped before the night patrol arrived. However, the mother was able to describe our distinct uniform, including the lavatory chains. In due course we were fined and lost shore leave. End of great international love affair.

The pantry boy job gave the opportunity for other escapades, mainly because we were in such close contact with the passengers. One of the lads looked rather like a gypsy, complete with earring, which was relatively unusual at that time. We told impressionable young women that he was a gypsy prince who could tell fortunes. This was a source of much fun, and clandestine visits to forbidden cabins, not to mention extra pocket money.

One of my favourite jobs as a pantry boy was to polish the floors of the corridors late at night using a large electric polisher. I found this very peaceful and satisfying work, while the majority of those on the ship were sleeping. There was a special knack to be learned when using the polisher, especially on a rolling ship. This involved pushing down on one side of the operating handle while lifting the other.

On one early evening I was operating the spinning brush at the top of the wide staircase leading to the first-class dining room. A sudden lurch of the ship caused me to lose control of the polisher. The machine dived down the stairs, dragging me with it and through the dining room doors. I finally brought it to a halt in the middle of the dining room under the thunderous gaze of the Chief Steward, surrounded by highly amused passengers.

The polishing machine seemed to be a centre of attraction for little old ladies, sometimes with a touch of tragedy. One first evening after leaving a port a new elderly lady passenger came and asked me, "When do we stop for the night, steward?" She did not seem

138

reassured when I explained that ships were well equipped to sail through the night. On another occasion we were almost an hour out from Melbourne in Australia when an elderly lady, who had come on board to see her friend off, asked of me, "Could you direct me to the gangway, please?" The sight later of the elderly lady clambering down the gangplank into the pilot cutter in a heavy swell would touch the heart of all sensitive sons.

Access to the polishing machine resulted in my first experience as an entrepreneur at sea. We regularly spent a full week in Sydney Harbour. All the passengers left the ship as she was prepared for the Pacific cruise on the outbound journey, and for a further week as we prepared to return home on the inbound trip. This was a time when the cabin stewards were required to thoroughly scrub the floors of their sections. But this was also an ideal time for many of them to spend extended visits with girlfriends they had established relationships with during the regular visits. My entrepreneurial skills helped me to exploit this situation.

During the daytime I would carry out my normal cleaning duties, but instead of going ashore at night I would use my machine to scrub the sections of the cabin stewards. And I would pay other boy ratings to go behind me and mop up. In this manner I was able to do the work of many cabin stewards over a few days. Often I would go for many days with almost no sleep.

The cabin stewards would pay me my asking price in Australian pounds, which at that time were 25 per cent lower than the English pound. I lent the Australian pounds I had earned to the other seamen as they ran out of funds during the extended stay in Sydney. They would then pay me back in English pounds at some predetermined port of call on the homeward voyage. This gave me a clear profit of 25 per cent. In ports such as Aden or Port Said, I would use the English pounds to buy items such as wristwatches, binoculars and music boxes to sell in Essex when I arrived home. Thus, I supplemented my meagre pay.

On one occasion, after the Suez Canal had reopened, my entrepreneurial activities were to get me into hot water. We were due to arrive at Port Said, where bargains were to be had. I was on duty in the passenger areas as we approached port. I watched the coastline draw slowly but ever closer into sight, while all around me passengers had swarmed on deck, laughing and chattering excitedly together, pointing to the shore ahead. As the ship began to lose speed I could see that the quay had lots of small brightly coloured boats bobbing around. These were "bum boats" waiting to tempt us with their wares.

A line of floating pontoons were used to connect the ship to the shore. The pontoons were lined by the many "bum boats" of locals selling their wares. I had no money at that particular time, but I had been told by an old "salt" that if I had anything that had a Union Jack on it this would be good for bargaining.

I took ashore a very old school gabardine raincoat, which proudly displayed a Union Jack on the label. I swapped the raincoat with one of the traders for a low stool in the form of a camel with a bright red leather cushion. As I came back on board one of the officers saw my stool and gave me a beautiful raincoat and asked me to carry out a similar bargain for him. I went back to the same trader, but he tried to give me back my old coat and keep the better one. I went berserk and before long the whole length of the pontoon was a mass of fighting seamen and traders. I was eventually dragged back on board by the Master at Arms (a kind of sea-going policeman) and peace was restored.

I was on one ship when they were making a film that was later to become very popular. It was called *The Captain's Table*, and I was to play a small part in it. The ship was anchored in the harbour of Gibraltar and passengers were being filmed being brought back to the ship in the liberty boats. My role was to stand on a gangplank down the side of the ship in full tropical uniform. As one of the liberty boats came alongside, one of the seamen was to throw me a rope from the boat, which I would deftly tie around the ship's rail to bring the boat to a smart halt. "If you don't know how to tie knots, tie lots of them," the quartermaster told me. As I struggled in interpretation of his stern advice he demonstrated, far too quickly, how to tie a hitch knot, or was it a tugboat knot?

The cameras were rolling, I caught the rope and quickly spun it round the ship's rail in what I assumed repeated the hitch knot the quartermaster had demonstrated for my benefit — but the boat sailed serenely on as my knot undid itself as swiftly as I tied it. End of film career! I was replaced in my coveted role, and every time I have seen the film since I have told all who will listen, "I was supposed to be in that".

Sometimes my ship would be in port with other liners from my home port of Tilbury. It was common practice to visit such ships to see if there were any crew members you knew. On one such visit I discovered a classmate from my school days. I was surprised to discover that, such a short time after leaving school, my friend had acquired a "posh" accent that he certainly didn't have when we were at school together. Perhaps the elevation in speech was promoted by the fact that he had a Lascar (a catch-all term assigned to any dark or dusky skinned sailor) to wait on him in the mess room.

It was not unusual to find our ship visited in port by men who had at some time in the past "jumped ship", that is, taken the opportunity to illegally stay in the country their ship was visiting. I met not less than four former school friends in this circumstance. The sad thing about them all was that they seemed to be in a kind of "no-man's land". They had some romantic attachments but, because they were illegal immigrants, they could not fully integrate into the community. They also had to limit their contact with friends on visiting ships, and relatives at home, for fear of being discovered by the authorities.

One such "ship jumper" from my home town came on board in New Zealand. He had made a new life for himself with a girlfriend, and was in regular employment and, therefore, liable to be deported if caught by the authorities. He asked me to visit his

142

mother, who worked in our local fish and chip shop, who he had not contacted since he had absconded. I was to assure her that he was well and happy. I found his mother's tears quite distressing when I eventually met her to convey his message.

CHAPTER
SIX

THE SCUM OF THE EARTH

During my five years in the Merchant Navy I came to realise that sailors are born romantics, prone to exaggeration, and have fluctuating moods and tempers. Although they argue and fight violently at times with each other, they summons a strange sense of loyalty when ashore and will dedicatedly protect a sworn enemy when he is threatened.

Many of the seafarers I met displayed almost Jekyll and Hyde characters. When off-duty whilst at sea they were slip-shod about their dress and swore profusely and continuously. But when they went ashore they dressed immaculately and rarely swore in front of women, not even the prostitutes who frequented the dock areas. For this reason there was outrage among seamen when a judge in the 1950s unfairly referred to them as, "The scum of the Earth" when sentencing a seaman for a crime. Certainly many seamen at that time had questionable morals, and excessive drinking habits, but most had a code of conduct and generosity that was rarely matched by their shore-bound counterparts.

144

Although many people do not look on seamen as particularly virtuous characters, I know from experience that many of them demonstrate acts of compassion to others. For example, while on leave and sitting in a London café on a bitterly cold day, eating pie and chips, a tramp came in and sat down with a cup of tea. He looked in a sorry state, other customers moved away from him, and the proprietor was looking as if he might evict him. But the seaman I was with got up, walked to the counter, bought two rounds of corned beef sandwiches, and put them down in front of the tramp without a word and came back and sat down. We then left the café without a word being passed. Life can be wonderful if you share it with others.

However, not all good deeds get the response they deserve. Although I have been guilty of oafish behaviour, I have always tried to show good manners. One day while sitting on a bus that was full, I stood up and offered my seat to a woman who was standing nearby. Instead of thanking me for my gesture, I was rewarded with a barrage of abuse for being a "sexist moron who stalked innocent women, and being responsible for keeping women down for centuries past." The woman made so much noise and embarrassment that I got off at the next stop, far from my intended destination, red with embarrassment.

During extended stays in ports such as Sydney, when all the passengers departed and the vessel was being made ready for the next ones, most of the crew took the opportunity to spend as much time ashore as possible. It was significant that a few seamen did not go ashore at all. These tended to be older members of the crew. I discussed this with one "old salt", who originally came from a town in north Essex. He amazed me with the fact that he had not been off the ship at all for four years. The ship was his only home and he had seen all our ports of call many times before and saw nothing new to entice him ashore.

An amazing coincidence occurred one day while sitting in the mess-room with two other boy ratings eating lunch. We all lived near each other at home in south Essex. We first noticed that we were all left handed — and holding the fork in the right hand when eating. A further coincidence was recognised when we discovered that we all had a girlfriend with the name of Stella (not a particularly common name at that time).

We quickly established that we were not all pursuing the same girl. Thereafter we would sit together composing our love letters which was the result of our combined effort. The now standard letters were to be posted at the next port of call. Then the ultimate coincidence occurred when we all received a "Dear John" letter from the three Stella's at the same port of call. One lad's letter was more unfortunate than the others. He had been sending identical letters to two girls and put them in the wrong envelope by mistake.

When I was sixteen years of age, I wasn't into alcohol or cigarettes, and, not being old enough, I had not been in a pub. We were docked in a port in New Zealand and a couple of kindly experienced seamen invited me to accompany them to a pub for a drink. I tagged along for the experience and, when I was asked what I would

146

like to drink, I answered, "Dunno, I've never been in a pub before and I don't know what drink I like." They kindly ordered a range of drinks for me to try, including the "green one" I said I thought "looked nice".

The idea was for me to sip each drink until I found one I felt comfortable with, and they would drink whatever I declined. I tried a mixture of beers and spirits, and one fiery spirit that I didn't like at all. On rejecting this drink I was then given a lecture on the venerable development of malt whisky, "twelve years ageing in sherry casks, then left in the dungeon of some ancient Highland castle, waiting for the time when some connoisseur would savour its magnificent flavour". My host then promptly tossed it back in one foul swoop without it even touching the sides of his taste buds. Who'd be a fine malt whisky?

I eventually settled on my youthful preference, créme de menthe (the "nice green stuff") with a Guinness chaser. This was just the right combination for an introduction into serious drinking. I passed out in the taxi on the way back to the ship and came back into the land of the living when we were well out to sea.

Although there was generally good camaraderie between shipmates, sometimes tempers flared. This is perhaps not surprising when so many men were closely confined in the tropical heat, in cabins close to the waterline. There were eight to twelve men in the crew cabins, and air conditioning was only provided for first-class passengers. I was myself involved in some fights for reasons that make no sense in the relative calm of normal life. But this was not normal life.

There were two petty officers called "Masters at Arms" whose job it was to police the lower decks. It was not a job that most would choose to do, but generally speaking they were obeyed and respected. But it happened that some altercations took place suddenly and without them knowing about it.

Most flare ups ended as quickly as they began, but a few became more serious. As a young boy I found these confrontations quite disturbing. Even as a boy at school I was not one to crowd round combatants when a fight began in the playground. On one occasion, two men locked themselves in their cabin determined to fight until one or the other was beaten senseless. Those of us outside the cabin didn't know what their argument was about, but the men were determined to settle it without outside interference.

Standing outside the cabin we could hear the men crashing about inside, the thud of blows and gasps of pain and curses. The Masters at Arms arrived but the combatants refused to respond to their shouts to open the cabin door, and we were left outside to await the outcome, whatever it might be.

The fight lasted about thirty minutes, but to those of us waiting outside it seemed much longer. Suddenly the door swung open. The sight inside the cabin was horrendous. One man was on his knees and even the victor could hardly keep on his feet. Both men had bleeding, puffed up faces and red knuckles. Although no weapons had been used the cabin, which slept eight men, was splattered with blood on every surface. The combatants were duly hauled off to the ship's hospital by the Masters at Arms. Later they were logged (fined) a week's wages by the Captain for the battle. The men got along fine after their fight. We never did find out what their grievance with each other was.

There were other dramatic battles. One of my ex-school friends appeared one day with badly swollen split lips. He had been in an argument with a very large sailor and it was clear that it was going to end in blows. To even up for his lack of size my friend grabbed hold of a large brass fire hose nozzle to hit the guy with. But in the time it took to get hold of the nozzle the man hit him with one mighty blow that floored him.

On another occasion I was told that my old friend Mr Golden Gloves had been involved in a fracas. He was a very quiet and mild man, but he wasn't someone I would have advised anyone to mix it with. And I was right. There had been a minor argument when he had complained to a cabin mate about hanging damp washing up to dry inside the cabin. His antagonist had attempted to hit him with a heavy glass beer mug. Unfortunately for him, his arm got caught in his own washing line before he could deliver the blow, and Mr Golden Gloves floored him with a single punch.

One of the saddest trips I made was on a very elderly liner called the *Orontes*. She was a beautiful vessel built on the now ancient traditional lines, similar to the *Titanic* but without the tendency to argue with icebergs. She had two corn coloured funnels set amidships, and a black hull, unlike the rest of the fleet to which she belonged, whose hulls were corn coloured, the same as their funnels. Her inside walls were of beautiful deep red-wood, and polished brass was in abundance. From the corridors of the cabin areas it was possible to look down on the splendour of the first-class dining saloon. Everything about the vessel had the aura of a bygone era. But this was her last trip. She was destined for the scrap yard. Every attempt was made to make her last voyage some kind of a celebration, but the atmosphere of impending doom remained with her throughout her final run back from Australia to England.

I found little commonality between ships officers. This appeared to have nothing to do with the type of ship. I served on posh ships where there were officers who were humane and others bumptious, and the same applied on smaller insignificant ships. I formed the opinion that the only justification for having some officers on ships at all was their capacity to issue non-essential orders to miscreants like myself in an attempt to keep them unnecessarily occupied.

I tended to give utmost respect to those officers I felt deserved it, irrespective of their rank. Conversely, those whom I felt abused their higher position I treated with as much disdain as I could display without getting into trouble.

On one passenger liner a junior purser was particularly arrogant, whereas his colleague of the same rank was polite and considerate. The polite one was always addressed with utmost deference in front of the passengers, whereas the other one who particularly tried to throw his weight around in front of young ladies found all sorts of misfortunes and misunderstandings followed his orders. Spilt coffee or soup was always in his lap.

On one cruise liner, on which I served for over a year, I was directly responsible to an officer for whom I had a lot of respect. I have always had an aversion to barbers and blood, especially my own blood! At one time my hair had grown unfashionably long. While in port in Hawaii, my officer said, "Don't you think it's time to get your haircut, Alan?" My regard for this officer was such that, rather than take offence to his suggestion, I decided to go ashore and take action. However, I had no money available. I visited a medical centre where they were offering a payment for people to donate blood. I used the money I earned to pay for the closest crop I have had in my life. When I arrived back on board my officer said, "Christ, Alan, I was suggesting a haircut, not a scalping."

Later, when I was to leave the liners and sail on smaller ships, I sailed on a small oil tanker where the First Officer insisted he was to be called "Sir". This was generally acceptable to me, but the manner of this man really aggravated me. Consequently, I made a point of calling him "Mr Mate" which was also unarguably correct. But I took great delight in referring to lower ranks of officers as "Sir" in his presence, which infuriated him.

He was a weedy, skinny bloke who looked ridiculous in the tropics when his legs stuck out from the bottom of his shorts like match sticks. I couldn't help notice how white his spindly legs were. Almost as white as his gleaming knee-length socks. First Officers obviously never sunbathe, but then, neither does God, I supposed, and they are more or less on the same par.

This officer was determined to exert his rank over me and looked forward to any opportunity to reprimand me. But I was too careful to slip up. One day he told me that the ship's "hospital is in a disgraceful state." It was the first time I realised that our small oil tanker had a "hospital". We certainly didn't have a doctor, or a nurse, to my dismay. I was shown this little room and instructed that the hospital was to be thoroughly cleaned, and if it was not hygienic when the officer inspected it later, I would be held to account. "Make sure you use plenty of disinfectant" was the final demand.

As far as I was concerned, he gave off about as much charm as a farmer who has just discovered a ferret up his trouser leg. I was determined to fix him, without getting into trouble of course.

We were in tropical waters and the heat and humidity was overpowering. But I made a superb job of cleaning the hospital. As a final measure I mopped the whole room with neat disinfectant. I then closed the portholes and the door, leaving the tropical heat to ferment the disinfectant. I then summoned said officer to inspect my work. By the time we arrived at the little room the tropical heat had done its work nicely. The officer opened the door and stepped sharply inside like a ferret (I waited at the door). The fumes that hit my adversary brought tears to his eyes and he came out quicker than he went in and beat a hasty retreat. But he never learnt, and we never got along. However, he wasn't smart enough to nail me as I knew he would have liked to.

It was while I was serving on a tiny oil tanker that I had need for medical attention. I had a large boil in the centre of the tip of my nose. This was causing me misery and discomfort. The person responsible for medical care of the ship was the chief steward, and I reported to him for treatment. He stood me against a wall in the corridor outside his cabin and presented me with a glass of rum, which I was instructed to down in one gulp. While my eyes were closed and smarting from the effect of the rum, he hit me with a smart smack on the nose, which promptly burst the boil. End of problem!

Having spent over three years on various ships, I had not spent a Christmas or birthday at home since I started my sea-going career. So, one November, I went to the shipping "pool" where seamen are assigned to ships and asked to be signed on a "coaster" that would enable me to get home in a couple of weeks time. I was assigned to the *British Rover* which I was told was doing a "run job" to Scandinavia — visit a couple of ports and return home in plenty of time for Christmas.

My allocated job on the *British Rover* was Captain's Tiger. I also looked after the Second Officer, who was a very amenable man. The Tiger's main task was to look after the Captain's domestic needs. This particularly involved keeping his living accommodation clean. That is, his day cabin and his night cabin; cleaning, changing linen, polish brass, etc., and to look after the Second

Officer in a similar way. In addition, the Tiger would ensure that the Captain was nourished when he had to spend long hours on the bridge, for example during extreme weather conditions.

The Captain of the *British Rover* was a superb officer, with a mild but authoritative nature that gained respect of all, except the Chief Engineer on this particular voyage. The Chief Engineer was frequently drunk. When he was in this state he would be openly discourteous to the Captain when they met, usually in the officers' dining salon. At these times I would feel overly protective of the Captain, although he was quite capable of dealing with the Chief Engineer in his own way.

It was not unusual for the Chief Engineer to be assisted back to his cabin to sleep off his drunken stupor by fellow officers, or even the stewards. I was pleased that I had not been allocated to look after his cabin. I would certainly have done a Captain Bligh on him, and cast him afloat in one of the lifeboats.

We arrived at one port and the Captain's wife had flown in to join the ship. This was not uncommon practice. She was a charming lady and we got on very well together. Far from increasing my workload, she reduced it, and she did so in a charming manner without interfering in any way.

It was some months before I touched England again. Unlike the liners, the *British Rover* did not have the precise timetable I had become accustomed to. She picked up oil in one port and took it to another. On one occasion we were in mid-Atlantic with a load of oil

154

when the Captain announced: "We're changing course for Hamburg (back in the direction we had come). They've sold the cargo." I found it difficult to comprehend that we could sail so many wasted days only to find we were retracing our route because the cargo had changed ownership while we were at sea.

At each port of call, rumours would fly around the ship that our next port was to be some exotic place (never home) but eventually we would learn that our destination was relatively mundane. We were in one port in a Norwegian fjord and ice formed around the ship thick enough for the locals to walk around the vessel. I had visions of being trapped in ice for many months, but we sailed without difficulty immediately our cargo had been off-loaded.

At the next port of call, in Sweden, we were loading a highly inflammable fuel. All the crew were called together in the recreation room which faced forward over the tanks. The portholes were open and the smell of the volatile cargo was drifting in. A senior officer was addressing us and explaining the danger of our new cargo and the care we should take. Some of the listening crew were smoking and as one of them finished his cigarette, he flicked his burning butt through the open porthole, in the manner that many did while we were relatively safe at sea. Those that had seen this happen dived to the deck in anticipation of a blast that fortunately was not to come. Shortly after this the whole crew were transferred to a local hotel while loading was completed. We subsequently proceeded to cause all the havoc that anyone could imagine would

155

ensue from placing a whole shipload of seamen in a hotel administered by beautiful young blonde chambermaids.

Our cargo was destined to be taken across the Atlantic to Texas, stopping en route in the Azores. I had formed a close friendship with two of the younger officers of the ship. Although their positions were superior to my own, I had far more sea-going experience. We decided to go ashore together, but had little money between us and we discussed what we could do that would be inexpensive but entertaining. They readily accepted my suggestion that we should visit a local brothel, survey the girls (for whom we had no money), accept the customary complimentary drink and make an excuse and leave. I had been initiated into this free entertainment by a very experienced sailor during my trips on the liners.

In due course we entered an appropriate house of "ill repute". The Madam paraded her girls and gave the three of us the customary glass of schnapps. This was when things began to go wrong. Three disturbingly large "minders" sidled into the room and it seemed likely that it would be less easy than we thought to extricate ourselves. Then I had a bright idea. We would start a fight between me and the radio officer whilst the electrician would try to intervene. My theory was that the brothel keepers would be keen to get us to leave and avoid the possibility of the police arriving. However, during the mock fight, we both pretended to head butt each other at the same time. I came off worse and was knocked out. I came to in a taxi on the way back to the ship. The ruse had worked, but I had a fearful headache.

We had to return to the ship by the motor lifeboat that had been lowered as a ship to shore tender for the few days we were in harbour and anchored offshore. With my painful head, the climb from the lifeboat up to the top of the accommodation ladder slung down the side of the ship was precarious to say the least. I no sooner got onto the ladder than the ship dipped and half of me, and my only shore-going suit, were immersed in sea water. My cabin mate met me at the top of the ladder and kindly informed me that I looked like a drowned rat.

Whilst in the Azores I made friends with some American Navy personnel. They took some of our crew to visit their shore base and entertained us cordially. In return for their hospitality we invited them back to our tiny oil tanker that was anchored in mid-harbour. The next day our liberty boat brought them out to the ship and we gave them a guided tour. After only a brief time they asked to be taken ashore again, declining our offer of a special meal we had prepared for them. When pressed for an explanation it turned out that they were seasick from the mild swell in the harbour. We were puzzled that fellow seamen should be affected in this way, but it materialised that this was the first time they had actually stood on the deck of a ship, as all their previous travel had been carried out by air.

Many months later I returned to the "pool" where I was allocated the ship. "I thought you were supposed to be giving me a coaster that was going to get me home for Christmas", I moaned. "I didn't say which coast, or which Christmas", was the unsympathetic retort by the shipping officer. We certainly got around on that trip.

I subsequently carried out many trips on oil tankers, often on small and insignificant vessels. But I found the fact that they rode so low in the water added to the excitement. It took only a relatively slight sea to cause their decks to be awash, something I had not experienced with liners.

One dark night I was on deck under the stars enjoying a warm breeze. As I looked towards the western horizon I saw a flash of lightning playing amid a distant bank of dark clouds, illuminating the dark mass with tawny gold.

The clouds drew nearer to the ship and the flashes became more numerous and distinct. In an instant it seemed as if the heavens were afire. After a long interval an answering rumble could be heard resounding towards the ship over the expanse of water.

Then with a single ear-splitting blast of thunder, almost as suddenly as they appeared, the fireworks display of lightning and the clouds disappeared like the end of an act in a play, leaving the stars to resume their calm display.

I shared a cabin on one very small oil tanker with a chap I had made several trips with on liners. He wore leather cowboy style boots all of the time. He occupied the lower bunk and I the top one in our two man cabin (a luxury following the cramped conditions of the liners). The manner of ventilation was a form of scoop that was stuck out of the porthole. This would scoop in air as the vessel moved along. The scoop could also catch a wave if one came too high, or the ship rolled too far. One night we were fast asleep, the ship rolled and the scoop brought in water with a rush and a bang like a cannon blast. We were soaked but dead tired. I could hear the water was splashing back and forth on the deck and realised that something would have to be done to rescue our belongings washing around below us. I heard my cabin mate stir on the lower bunk, curse and get out of bed. He will deal with it, I thought. But he just picked up his boots, put them on top of a locker to dry, and went straight back to sleep, leaving all our other belongings floating around on the deck.

It was whilst on one such small tanker ship that, on Christmas Day, one of the typical Atlantic storms overtook us. The weather began to deteriorate, with a rough sea, low cloud, and visibility falling quickly. The radio gave us not only the weather forecast, but also the shipping forecast. It was not good. Experienced seamen don't acknowledge the force of the wind until it is past force seven. Up to that point they talk of it as, "It's a bit of a blow". At force nine it became difficult to stand up on the outside deck, away from the comfort of the crew's quarters. Soon the storm was rising towards force eleven on the Beaufort scale, and we were in trouble.

Suddenly the whole seascape changed. Now, under the low grey sky, through the driving rain and spray, the whole sea was white — a vast creaming expanse as far as the eye could see. I had seen the Australian Bight and the Bay of Biscay at their worst; they were nothing

159

compared to this. It was like gazing on a wild mountainous landscape, but the whole scene was in majestic motion.

The gale hit us with a vengeance; it was as if we were being tossed between enormous, moving mountains. There are few more stirring experiences than being aboard a ship in a gale, especially a low-riding vessel such as a small oil tanker. She is pounded by the wind and bucks like a wild thing as she ploughs through mighty seas. Although I had experienced storms on passenger liners, their effect on a small oil tanker was far more dramatic because they lie so low in the water.

As the day wore on the crests and troughs became enormously greater; now further apart; the crests began to curl over, breaking as they came with an avalanche of foam streaming down the steep cliff of the waves. At one time I found my eyes drawn to a particularly ominous-looking grey green wall of a wave towering and running towards us, a beard of wind-torn foam flying before it. I felt the ship slightly alter course to deflect the force of the blow, dividing the onslaught to smother the ship in foam and solid water.

The ship rolled and pitched violently. Far from being frightened I found the experience so exhilarating that for a while I went to the upper deck at the aft end to watch the ship tussle with the wildest seas I had ever experienced. Everywhere I could see the swollen sea running at us in fury and, it seemed to me, without direction. I took some photos with an ancient brownie camera that showed the spray from the waves hitting the ship's funnel. How I wished that I had a better

160

camera to more faithfully record the drama taking place.

Rank on rank of great combers battered our labouring ship which was being forced almost broadside to the gale. The waves burst in fury over the side rails, white water washing along the exposed deck and roaring out of the scuppers back to the sea. One moment the ship was lifted up towards the lowering clouds and then she was dashed down into the valley of the trough, sending a shuddering shock through her.

Waves were breaking over the bow and the aftermath of the blow shot spray as high as the bridge amidships. The tops of the oil tanks were at times swamped with water as high as the catwalk that connected the after end of the ship with the amidships officers quarters. Later I would be required to negotiate this plunging catwalk to take food from the galley to the amidships dining salon.

The storm continued in full fury all day. My task was to carry warm food to the officers on the bridge. Too soon the time came for me to run the gauntlet of the sea-battered catwalk from the stern of the ship to the mid-ship area where the bridge was positioned. In the middle of the catwalk there was a safety arch. I planned to start my oilskin clad run as the ship rose from the trough of the sea. I would then shelter in the relative safety of the arch during the next dip beneath the waves, and run the second section as she rose again. I made two journeys in this manner. Before my third attempt, part of the catwalk disappeared, smashed away by the fury of the sea. This made it impossible to carry hot food from the galley at the after end to the officers' quarters amidships. The officers had to survive on sandwiches from thereon until the storm abated several days later.

Eventually the ship hove to, and turned to face the onslaught, to ride out what had turned into a force eleven gale, and to enjoy a relatively more comfortable ride. This was how I spent my fourth Christmas, and my birthday, at sea. In time we limped into Hamburg to lick our wounds, make repairs, discharge our cargo, and to take on much needed stores for the next leg of our journey to England, at last.

For some time I had held doubts about life at sea. Whilst the times in port were full of activity the periods at sea often seemed without purpose once the novelty had worn off. The long sameness of the days began to cause me to question whether it was time to move in a new direction. I put this feeling to a long-serving seaman and his response was, "Look at the set up I've got here. No worries, no wife, no mother-in-law, food whenever I want it. All I have to do is turn to on time, run around for a few snotty-nosed officers making them feel important, and the rest of the time is mine. I've got it made". For Tom, the ship was his home and his family. But my doubts remained about how long I wanted to sail the seas.

It was while serving on an oil tanker that I began to realise that I had an academic ability I had not recognised. I had always spent a lot of time reading on ships. Although this reading did not include the

162

classics, I tended to avoid the trash that so many seamen appeared to find of interest.

I discovered a desire to read at greater depth, and this has remained with me ever since. I enrolled for two correspondence courses organised especially for seamen. One was for English and the other in Physics. Later I added an art course. I would receive a programme of reading with follow up exercises which I returned for assessment.

Whilst completing a physics module, I was unsure if I was interpreting a particular procedure correctly and approached various officers for advice, including the Captain and the Chief Engineer. None could help with the level I was at. As a consequence of this event the Captain had a discussion with me that was to cause me to consider abandoning life at sea. He insisted that I was wasting my time in the Merchant Navy and that I should go ashore to develop my academic ability to the full. I wasn't entirely convinced of this, but it did give me something to think about.

For some time I had been suffering from increasing deafness and this seemed the right time to go ashore and get something done about it, and also to take the opportunity to think about moving in a new direction.

CHAPTER
SEVEN

A CHANGE OF
DIRECTION

I initially looked at my move away from the happy-go-lucky sea-going life as a temporary transition period. My intention was to take a shore job while I underwent the operations necessary to correct my hearing loss, and I would then return to the carefree way of life I had been enjoying. But reality was to prove different. I was never to return to shipboard life, and several important coincidences were to shape my future development.

Many people I knew from my home town travelled to East Tilbury to work at the Bata shoe factory. I decided to apply for work there while I sorted out my medical problems. They had a reasonably paid vacancy in their warehouse and I put in a request for this position. But the coincidence of taking a test that I had not anticipated resulted in a move in a different direction.

I attended an interview in the Personnel Department and completed a series of tests. Following the analysis of the aptitude tests, the company Personnel Manager suggested to me that the results of the tests I had taken indicated that I would be wasted in warehouse work. He offered me the more attractive post of Assistant Contracts Manager in the Wholesale Sales Department. The job specification for the office job included the words, "The applicant should be career minded". I took this to mean there would be a need to crawl and grovel (I wasn't far wrong).

Whilst the office job had the greater prestige value, and the working environment was more attractive than the warehouse, the pay was some 25 per cent lower than the warehouse work. Although I intended the job would be an interim one, and I certainly didn't look on it as a career move, I decided to take the lower paid job, and in retrospect this proved to be a good decision.

An important part of the work I was undertaking involved bidding by tender for contracts to supply footwear to government departments. Where the tenders were successful, resulting in the award of a contract, I would then ensure that the factories produced the products in time for supply to the various ordnance depots.

The Bata Shoe Company had its origins in people fleeing from Nazi occupation of Czechoslovakia during the Second World War. Consequently, all the top management were Czech and had a distinct foreign accent. Whilst I found this accent quite pleasant, I found it absolutely hilarious to hear English middle managers, who wanted to ingratiate themselves with top management, talking in Pidgin English. One such manager had an oil painting of himself in his office. The artist clearly didn't like him much.

165

On one occasion I went to see my English group manager to ask his advice on a particular aspect of a tender I was working on. The question I put to the manager clearly took him out of his depth, but his response made me giggle to myself. "Whitcomb," he said, "I am just simple country turnip, I no can answer such words you say. I say you go think yourself and do what you think." I was astounded to hear this level of language from an English group manager. This man (and so many others in the firm) clearly thought that this manner of speaking endeared him in some way to his Czech superiors, but my own experience of the top management of the company gave me no impression that they expected or respected an approach such as this. As Mark Twain said, "It's better to keep your mouth shut and appear stupid than to open it and remove all doubt."

For a while I rented a small flat on the Bata housing estate. I say a flat, but really it was a small room. In fact the room was so small that when I turned the light off I could get into the bed before the room got dark. However, there were plenty of distractions that went with the accommodation. There were also young girls in nearby flats. They were over in England from countries such as Spain, Italy and Malta to work in Bata's factories. They were generally very pretty girls and they would visit my flat and offer to do washing and ironing and provide snacks, which was very acceptable to a young lad.

I eventually spent five years working for this company and, although some of their business practices were somewhat eccentric, I was on a continuous upward learning curve throughout my employment there, and many of the business efficiency skills learnt while with the company have continued to prove useful.

My work, as I have said, involved tendering for contracts with central and local government, and other major organisations large enough to order sufficient quantities of footwear to finance their own production runs. I would tender for footwear supplies to the Army, the Royal Navy, the Royal Air Force, the Post Office, and the Atomic Energy Authority and also to education authorities for the supply of plimsolls for schools. I would then supervise production and delivery schedules when a contract was established.

Dealing with government tenders was very complicated because the specifications for manufacture that they laid down were very demanding to meet, and the delivery schedule had to be strictly adhered to. When a tender resulted in a contract it meant a lot of welcome work for the factory units situated on the same site as my office. The next part of my work involved advising the factory managers of the success of the tender, which was a pleasant chore to carry out. My next task was to ensure that the production and delivery schedule within the contract were met. These were "white coat" jobs.

The normal attire expected for work in the office was a formal suit and tie. But for visits to the factories the "done thing" was to put on a white coat to cover the suit. Quite apart from the practicality of protecting the suit in the factory visit, there was a message in the

167

ritual. Workers in the factory had their own code of dress. Production line workers did not wear overalls; foremen had brown overalls, while the factory managers had white coats. My white coat had a message that said, "I'm important, I'm from the office and I wear a suit. I have to have a white coat to protect my clothes when entering your domain. But notice how smart and sharp my white coat is."

Although there was an element of implied snobbery in this white coat business and the position I held, my reception on the production lines was always hospitable. This was especially so when I came to announce the arrival of a new large contract. On such occasions I was elevated to celebrity status, and, for a young man, this boosted my ego.

Needless to say, not all contracts went according to plan. On one occasion, I was summoned to the Army Central Ordnance Depot to examine a major problem with the large contract of leather shoes the company was supplying. We were halfway through the production run and the "problem" had only just come to light.

On arrival at the depot I was taken through various warehouses, where my guide pointed out the products of other suppliers. At one point he indicated a very large block of stacked boxes, which he said contained "manhole covers" (in a clothing warehouse?). It took some time before I realised that the "manhole covers" were in fact service women's knickers!

When I arrived at the footwear section the problem was painfully obvious. Many shoes supplied had nails sticking through the soles. The speed and volume of our production meant that a major inspection operation would have to be undertaken, followed by repairs to rectify the situation. My elderly guide sternly reprimanded me, "Do you realise, young man, if there was a war on, you'd be charged with sabotage?" I tried to look suitably horrified while chuckling to myself.

I had by now begun to investigate what could be done about my hearing loss. At the first hospital consultation I was told that it was possible to do something to repair my ear drums, but first my nose would have to be repaired. My nose had been broken in two places through boxing and, although I quite liked its distorted, flattened state, it was preventing me from breathing properly.

I had a nose job that would probably have cost a small fortune had I been required to pay for it. The finished product was certainly straighter, and I could breathe better, but I did prefer the old model. However, having solved the nose problem it was now possible to attempt to repair the damage to my ear drums.

Although both of my ear drums were damaged the hearing loss in my right ear was hardly noticeable — it was by far my better ear. So, I was surprised that the surgeon chose to operate on my right ear first. But, like so many medical patients, I did not consider questioning the plans.

I was to embark on a number of operations, first on one ear and then the other. The strategy involved trying to take grafts from veins to attempt to repair the perforations. The operations were not successful, but the disaster for me was that I became completely deaf in my right ear, and the hearing loss in my left ear remained severe. This hearing loss has challenged me ever since.

It was during my work for the shoe manufacturing company, and during the time of the earliest of my ear operations, that I met the girl who was to become my wife, Olivia. We met by an important coincidence. I happened to attend the annual works dinner of a small local company where Olivia's mother worked. I knew her mother already, but did not know she had a gorgeous daughter. Olivia was there with her longstanding boyfriend. I was allocated a place on the same table as Olivia, her family, and her boyfriend. I swapped my sweet (I rarely ate sweet things) for her coffee (and she didn't drink coffee).

For me it was love at first sight. For Olivia, it took much longer, and a lot of pestering before she was to come around to recognising that we were well suited. Her reluctance was understandable considering my poor track record, with many girlfriends, and the supposed reputation of most sailors. I am sure that the reputation of sailors is grossly exaggerated, but there is some truth attached to them also.

When I finally persuaded Olivia to drop her current boyfriend and come out with me on a date, I enthusiastically waited for the chosen day. Unfortunately, the day before the date she was taken ill. Wanting to impress her, I sent some flowers. When she recovered and we eventually got to go out on a proper date, she never mentioned the flowers. After some subtle prompting, it turned out that the flowers had never

170

been delivered. So, I went to the florist to find out what had happened. Investigations finally revealed that the flowers had been delivered to the funeral of a neighbour. As if this was not bad enough, the card I had written out read, "Sorry you're not feeling so good. But enjoy the flowers anyway. Better luck next time." I hate to think what the family of the deceased thought!

During the time we were courting, I owned a pretty new and "trendy" car. I asked Olivia if she would like to learn to drive. She said, "Yes", and we arranged a date to start her lessons. But before the date arrived, I sold my shiny dream car and bought an old banger. This was love, but not that loving to ruin a sweet gearbox! Not surprisingly, Olivia did not look overjoyed when I turned up to take her out for her first driving lesson.

We married in a relatively short period of time, and we started married life in a flat provided by the shoe company, until we had saved enough for a deposit on a home of our own. I soon found that Olivia is brilliant at knitting. She's not very good at checking if the car is running out of petrol, or pumping up the tyres now and then, but she's brilliant at knitting. She can take a page of instructions that resemble Einstein's calculations on the theory of relativity and turn it into a beautiful sweater. She also turned out to be a brilliant navigator on long journeys, although she does have the infuriating habit of saying, "You've got to go that way." But she's also very pretty, so I forgive her that.

When my wife was due to give birth to each of our two daughters, I was quite horrified that she was to have them in our own home, and even more distressed to learn that she wanted me present at the births. I was squeamish and anxious, and certainly did not want to be present at either of the births. I felt that a hospital was the right place for births to take place, and I wasn't comforted by being told that some women give birth quite alone out in the bush or in the jungle. However, Olivia had the last word when she demanded, "You were there at the beginning, and I expect you to be there at the end." And so I was present. I would like to be able to say it was an exhilarating experience, but in reality it was full of apprehension for me. I am quite willing to admit that I am one of those men who would not like to go through childbirth.

After our second daughter, Jo-Anne, was born, I spent a long time trying to impress on our eldest daughter, Lisa-Jane, the importance of first aid. I took the time to emphasise the importance of taking the right action quickly. Then I asked her seriously, "What would you do if your sister swallows the door key?" Her answer was, "I'd climb in through the window." Makes sense!

As part of an economy drive, and to help Lisa-Jane finance her Christmas shopping one year, Olivia and I offered her 5p for every local Christmas card she delivered. She got it a bit wrong and went around asking for 5p for each one. She came back from her first deliveries with 27p. One lady only gave her 2p because that was all the change she had, and six said they had enough already thank you.

As Lisa became older she became quite pedantic when people too frequently spelt her name with a Z rather than an S. I was with her one day when we opened her first bank account. I gave the bank clerk her Christian name as "Lisa" and she quickly interjected, "With an S." The clerk then asked, "Do you spell your surname with a double S?" I said, "But I haven't told you our surname yet." "But you have", she said, "Your daughter said it is Withaness."

When Jo-Anne was about four years of age, I watched her from a distance, apparently talking and gesticulating to a non-existent person. Thinking it was an imaginary friend (such as one her elder sister talked to openly), I asked her who she was talking to. "Why, Daddy, it's the pretty lady of course. She comes to see me every night." Many years later I became very interested in the paranormal, but at that time I found it a bit eerie to hear my young daughter speak of such things. "Aren't you afraid of the lady?" I asked. Jo-Anne looked at me as if she was talking to an idiot. "Of course not, Daddy, she's lovely, and she wears beautiful dresses." Not long after this I attended a spiritualist church for the first time ever. The visiting medium said to me, "There's a spiritual presence in your house. You should not be afraid. She is a good spirit." Coincidence? Maybe!

It was about the time of the birth of our children that I seemed to take over the cooking in our house. I'm not really sure how this came about. It may have started when I asked my wife to prepare some dripping toast, and she put butter on before adding the dripping. Yuk! But it is more likely that my cooking duties materialised at the time when the children were very young. During nappy changing sessions I would be asked, "I'm up to my arms in 'it' at the moment, be a dear and check the spuds." One certainly doesn't want someone up to their arms in "it" messing around with food. From then on I became increasingly involved in cooking.

To be fair, I really do enjoy the cut and thrust of kitchen warfare, and I am forever collecting interesting recipes. But if the truth were to be known, I rarely refer to recipes. I tend to literally throw things together, and even make it up as I go along. On the one hand the dishes are not time consuming to prepare, but on the other hand they are never consistently the same. I have several versions of corned beef hash, and I can produce real mean fried rice in a thousand and one variations, and I don't think one has yet been repeated exactly.

One virtue my wife has, that I would dearly like her to teach me, is how to deal with the many wild animals that invade our home. Whereas my answer to any invasion is murder, she has a much more humane approach than me. My wife quickly learnt that a scream from me in the bathroom means that I have been trapped by a marauding spider with deadly venom. The scream is to summon her to run to my rescue, gently pick up the spider (that is now stone deaf as a result of my screams for help) and take it out into the garden, so that it can creep back in and terrorise me again at some unguarded moment. And all this is to prevent me from doing the most sensible thing, i.e. jump up and down on it.

I don't know where this aversion to spiders originated for me. I put it down to visits from Great

Aunt Violet and other old ladies when I was a kid. I knew that when old ladies came to visit I was expected to kiss them. Even today I can't understand why old ladies expect little boys to want to kiss them. Especially little boys with permanently sticky lips, and an obvious abhorrence to kissing anyone, let alone hairy old ladies.

Great Aunt Violet was rather hairy and I used to dread her visits, even though a kiss was rewarded with half-a-crown. The main problem was her moustache which literally seemed to quiver as I got close to do the business. I had a nightmare following one such visit. In the nightmare I had to kiss a whole row of Great Aunts. As I approached to do my duty to Aunt Violet her moustache turned into a spider, and I've been afraid of spiders ever since. But why does my beloved have to rescue me from moths also? Maybe both these aversions go back to the family hut we lived in when hop picking.

My wife is an excellent driver. I have to admit she drives a lot more calmly than I do. She says that my main problem is my right foot. It looks normal enough but she swears that it is made of lead, and as I have grown older and weaker I have not got the strength to stop it going into free fall on the accelerator. I don't think I really drive fast because people seem to go by us like we are standing still. But recently I did get a photo sent to me by a nice police photographer, showing that I was doing forty seven miles an hour in a forty mile an hour zone. Now, whilst I don't particularly object to the £60 fine imposed in exchange for my photo, I do object to the three points put on my driving licence. I have

175

been driving for well over forty years, without so much as a parking ticket, and now I am a marked man for the next three years. But when I phoned the police at a time when my property was being attacked by vandals, it took more than an hour and half for a policeman to arrive, on a bike.

Having said all this, cars do not rate very highly in my list of priorities. I have never been able to fathom out why so many people, particularly men, seem to attach so much importance to their cars. I have friends, one of whom owns a red Ferrari, and one who owns a red Porsche (what's with men and red sports cars?). I've ridden in both of my friends' cars and neither impresses me, but they are very high in their list of priorities.

It was during my working time with the shoe company that I began to practice judo. I was fortunate to have two friends who were black belt judo players. Black belts were relatively rare in Britain at that time and almost a rarity in Essex. One of my friends was the heavyweight champion and in the British national team, so for my introduction to the sport I had the ideal guides.

Encouraged by my friends to attend training sessions, I took to judo naturally. I was immediately more successful than I had been in the art of boxing. I found it pleasing that I did not get hurt in the way that I always did when I was boxing, and I was in the privileged position to be able to train with several members of the national squad.

My progress through the grades of coloured belts was relatively rapid, and I had a small collection of favourite techniques that knocked over most of my opponents, no matter how big they were, although I was often at a disadvantage when fighting on the ground where I was not that strong. I particularly preferred to fight much heavier opponents, probably because, although they were stronger than me, they tended to be slower movers.

Although my progress through the coloured belts was pretty quick, the later and most important stage, resulting in the opportunity to contest for the coveted black belt, was understandably arduous. Today it is possible to achieve the grade of black belt through a cumulative points system. Points can be accumulated by fighting other equivalent grades of players (those also holding the grade of brown belt). This point can be won at official grading contests, or at important events such as championships. When sufficient points are gained, the grade of black belt (First Dan — the first grade of black belt) is awarded.

At the time when I was contesting for the grade of black belt the system was far more demanding than it is today. A collection of holders of the grade of brown belt were gathered together at a grading session. These players would contest each other in individual contests. Those achieving the highest number of wins were given the honour of a "line up". Eight brown belts would be lined up and the candidates for the grade of black belt would face the line and fight each person one after the other. The minimum of achievement for promotion to the grade of black belt was six wins.

The day I gained the grade of black belt was truly exciting. There came the terrifying time when I reached the stage of the line up. I stood facing several of my opponents and knew that each of them also wanted to do well, and then came the exhilaration of knowing that the person you had just turned over has resulted in you achieving the coveted award of First Dan. Later I was to successfully compete for the second grade of black belt (Second Dan). For this grade a similar process was followed as that for First Dan, except that in this case the line up consisted of black belts. I know of nothing more intimidating than facing a line up of eight black belt players, all of whom are contesting for the same honour. Towards the end of the line up of fights, when I was truly "cream crackered", I would hope that when I turned my opponent over, it would be a clean throw ending the contest, or that he would go down, and stay down.

I participated in the judo championships on several occasions at Crystal Palace and other important venues. I was never spectacularly successful, although I did pick up a few medals and other trophies. One thing about my experience of participating in the champion-ships was that I had no problems in remaining within my weight category. While other contestants would have to run around the block wrapped in polythene or wearing a rubber suit prior to "weighing in", I could calmly sit munching a chocolate bar. Similar to my experience when boxing, nothing would encourage my weight to rise above the lightweight category.

With the passing of time I felt the need to move on from the work I was doing with the shoe company. But I was unsure what next stage in my personal development I wanted to pursue. The scope of possibilities open to me was limited because I held no formal qualifications, having left school at the age of fifteen without sitting for any examinations, other than to have failed the dreaded Eleven-Plus. Then I saw an advertisement in a local newspaper where a business-man was inviting someone to join his small manufacturing company as a partner, to provide capital for expansion of the business. The savings that Olivia and I had amounted was just the sum that this man was seeking, and we decided that I should leave my job and join him.

It took only a very short time in the partnership to realise that things were not right. Although there was a small factory producing children's educational toys and board games, the workers' wages were not being paid regularly, and when I made a few enquiries it appeared that their National Insurance contributions were not being paid either. It was also clear that there were no customers for the products that the business was turning out, and the vehicles the business was operating were not being paid for. My new partner was clearly as reliable as an ice cube in a sauna.

Suspecting that there was a fraud operation going on, I contacted the police. I was advised that my partner was already under investigation for a string of fraudulent activities, using a number of aliases. I was asked not to alert him until the trap could be sprung to ensnare him. During this waiting period I not only had to continue to live with little income, other than the small amount I was earning from judo, to meet my mortgage commitments and support my family, I also had to witness the sufferings of our small workforce who were working without pay.

In due course my "partner" was arrested, put on trial, and found guilty of fraud, for which he was sentenced to four years imprisonment, while his victims, including myself and my family, had to pick up their lives and try to rebuild them. This was far easier said than done, but sad though this event was, it marked an important turning point in my life.

The initial difficulty for me was that, because I had theoretically been self-employed, I was not entitled to unemployment benefit. During this time of hardship Olivia and I did "outwork" in our own home, for a pittance, in order to feed ourselves and our children. Our mortgage was put on temporary hold and we paid only the interest and not the capital. The "out work" we took on included painting tiny ornaments, packing ladies' paper knickers in bags, and putting medical spatulas into their packets, and we packed buttons; the list was almost unending. When Christmas came we were thankful to tour the charity shops and buy second-hand toys that we could renovate for our children. All our Christmas decorations were homemade.

During this time of extreme hardship our two young daughters were a source of support to us. They never complained about the lack of material things, or the fact that we used to have to call them indoors when the ice cream man came down the road, playing his cheerful tune to summon other youngsters to come running to buy an ice cream. But, nevertheless, this was a period in our lives that was very hard, and the experience of this hardship has never been forgotten.

I eventually found new employment, but I wasn't back in work more than six months when I parted company with my new employers through no fault of my own. I was just caught up in the numbers game, and I felt a deep sense of injustice and loss of self-esteem. Once more the spectre of the dole hovered like an incessant moth.

While I had been employed in business I learnt that old maxim, "Where there is a demand, supply it. Where there isn't one, create it." This saying is at the heart of most cut-throat commercial practice. But, needless to say, I could find no one to supply money when my need was so great while unemployed. There was the dole of course, but that only helped us to survive at the very most, and I had to resort to other methods to give my young family some resemblance of normal life.

It was during these hard times of unemployment that a local builder offered me £10 to dig a hole. At the time this seemed too good an opportunity to miss for a bit of cash. My benefactor took me to a road, drew a square in the pavement in chalk and said, "Dig down until you get to some pipes, mate" and left me with a spade and a pick-axe.

I had in the past struggled to dig a hole in my relatively soft garden. I had never even held a pick-axe before. But these were desperate times for me. I was picking away at the pavement and getting nowhere when two hefty guys came along and started watching, making ribald comments about my pansy actions. Eventually they took pity on my predicament, grabbed the pick-axe in turns and broke through the concrete to the earth below. To reach this stage took two hours of my labour, but only thirty minutes once I had the assistance of my "helpers".

Now I was through to the softer earth below the going got a little easier, but not much. The hole in the concrete was too small to get into, so I had to dig and scoop the earth out. After another three hours I came to a pipe. Five hours after having started on my £10 job I had reached the important goal, and I rushed quickly to the site where my benefactor was working to convey the good news. He came and inspected my hole and exclaimed, "Sorry mate, that pipe's the wrong colour, but if you dig a bit lower you'll come to another one. Let me know when you get there. And please stop hanging about. I need that hole today you know!"

And so I dug on, now encumbered by the position of the pipe I had uncovered. I did eventually expose the pipe of the "right colour" and collected my £10 reward. I arrived home eight hours after leaving on my expedition as a navvy with the most terrible blisters on my hands, that took two weeks to heal. Since then I have had nothing but admiration for men who do this kind of work.

In retrospect the period of hardship while I was unemployed had the important effect of spurring me to move in a different direction that was to change my life for the better forever. However, at the time it was a worrying period of uncertainty and self doubt.

I was unemployed for a complete year. I found this a very dispiriting experience and, quite apart from the financial difficulties we faced, my self-esteem plummeted. Every week I would apply for numerous jobs by letter, expending some of our limited money on stationery and postage stamps that we could ill-afford. Many potential employers did not even have the courtesy to acknowledge my letter. Sometimes an official application form would arrive to be filled in. It was these forms that brought home to me my lack of formal qualifications, because I couldn't include anything in the qualifications section. It was clear that without such qualifications the future looked black for me and my family. I decided that I needed to obtain qualifications, but the question was, how?

After a year of unemployment I eventually obtained a job in an office in central London, which meant finding the fare to travel to and from London each day. Because the work was not well paid, after having taken into account the cost of travel, I was no better off working than on the dole. But my morale was lifted considerably and by teaching judo in the evenings and at weekends, our standard of living began to slowly improve. My wife also took part-time employment while my mother-in-law minded our two children. In this way we began to get back on our feet.

I was determined that I would never draw dole again. I knew that the only way of ensuring this was to secure a safer form of employment, and this meant obtaining some qualified status. However, I was under the misapprehension that failure at the time of the Eleven-Plus examination prevented me from academic progress along that route. I realised that evening classes existed but assumed they were aimed at practical skills, and I had no illusions that this was a direction where I would not be successful.

As I have mentioned in an earlier chapter, a significant event in my schooling was taking the Eleven-Plus examination which, if I passed, could have resulted in me going to a grammar school. This was something that I was keen to happen. I received no special coaching for the examination but, as I was regularly second or third position in the top class of the school, it was generally expected that I would pass with relative ease. This was not to be the case.

I have also related in an earlier chapter the circumstances whereby, although I theoretically passed the Eleven-Plus, I ended up in a "pool" of those whose scores were slightly lower than others who had directly obtained an assured place in one of the several grammar schools. I realised that the result was probably caused by my tendency to rush through tests and make silly errors, but I felt disappointed by what I saw as an unfair situation. Consequently, I attended the interview with a poor attitude and I was not successful. The final straw came when a woman asked what kind of books I liked, and when I reeled off some of the respectable ones she asked the names of the authors and my mind went completely blank. Then she asked about my preferred music and I pronounced Beethoven with "Beat . . ." as opposed to "Bate . . ." and I knew I had blown it. End of interview.

My annoyance at the apparent disparity of educational opportunity stayed with me for a long time after the Eleven-Plus stage of my education. Many years later I was to learn that Winston Churchill once said that "Exams always asked me questions about things I didn't know, rather than asking about what I did know." This reflected my attitude towards examinations for many years following my disappointment with the Eleven-Plus outcome, and coloured my feelings about examinations for a very long time.

Following the Eleven-Plus experience, I was left with the impression that because I had failed the Eleven-Plus examination, access to "O" levels was blocked. It was to take a coincidental meeting to dispel this misapprehension. This meeting was to change the direction of my life.

During my year of unemployment I worked in a couple of youth centres teaching judo to youngsters of varying ages, but mainly teenagers. I realised that I seemed to have an affinity with young people, and even older kids from a local detention centre. About this time I met a lecturer from London University who was involved in the training of teachers. He was familiar with my work with youngsters and suggested that I should undertake a teacher training course, for which the entry level at that time was five GCE "O" levels. I

185

explained to this man that I could not obtain the necessary "O" levels because I had failed the Eleven-Plus examination. He enlightened me that attainment of the qualifications I needed was not dependent on Eleven-Plus success. In retrospect I am amazed at my ignorance!

CHAPTER EIGHT

THE LAW OF AVERAGES

Although the revelation that the Eleven-Plus outcome did not preclude me from sitting examinations was encouraging, the achievement of five "O" level passes still seemed daunting. I had never sat a formal examination before, apart from the fateful Eleven-Plus. I knew that formal examinations were the way forward for me, but there was another particular difficulty for me to overcome. Although I had the office job in London during the day, because the pay was so poor, I still needed to teach judo in the evenings to earn enough money to give my family more than the bare necessities. We were also trying to catch up the back payments on our mortgage. I didn't feel it was fair for my family to make even greater sacrifices — they had suffered enough! So, I needed to find a way to begin obtaining my initial qualifications without attending evening classes — a seemingly impossible task.

The answer to my dilemma lay in the studies of a fellow traveller on the train to and from Essex into London. I noticed that my companion was always furtively reading sheets of paper and scribbling notes. It transpired that he was studying for three GCE "O" levels through part-time day-release provided by his employers. He was studying economics, office practice and commerce. Reading his notes and text books I realised that much of what he was studying was already very familiar to me from my work with the shoe company several years back. I just needed the language and theory to accompany my previous experience. I could teach myself the subject matter.

I began photocopying my travelling companion's notes he had made following his classes, and in this way forming my own set of theoretical notes. I also bought the course texts he was studying. Towards the end of his course I purchased sets of past examinations papers and practiced writing answers to the questions set. Although I had no tutor to assess and mark my work and give me feedback, I became confident that I could make a good stab at the exams.

I also found a local evening class for English language that was running on the one evening when I was not doing judo, so I enrolled for that. The English tutor was a huge Welshman named Davies whose enthusiasm recognised no boundaries. He was just the inspiration I needed. I was frank with him about my limited academic success and my desperate need to obtain some "O" levels, quickly! His eloquent classroom speeches motivated me and the other mature students in the class. I avidly accepted and tackled the many assignments he set and, even when my work had missed the target, his constructive criticism only served to inspire me further.

188

Mr Davies taught me how to use words and to enjoy literature. It was an excellent experience to listen to such an articulate and stimulating teacher. When he read to us he did it so movingly that he conveyed us to a different world. I devoured the reading he recommended. I read them in all sorts of places and at all sorts of times. Visits to the toilet were invaluable! I savoured all that I was reading and nothing was wasted on me.

I was twenty-seven when I went back to school. My family understood what I was trying to do. Although my judo friends thought I had gone a bit soft in the head, learning was heady stuff for someone starved of learning for so long. The only thing that slightly spoiled this wonderful new experience was the urgency of knowing the main purpose was to obtain the examination passes needed to gain entry to teacher training college as soon as possible.

Even though I felt sure that I had covered the content of each of the syllabuses, as the time approached for examination entry I felt far from confident. I decided to adopt the "law of averages strategy", which was really a haphazard concept of my own. Surmising that I couldn't hope to be successful in all four subjects, I elected to enter for each of the four subjects with three different examination boards — twelve examinations for the four subjects. The assumption being that I would fail some and pass some, and my "law of averages" would hopefully give me the four separate subject passes I was aiming for.

I was due time off work for holidays and took this during examination time. I spent a frantic time dashing from one examination centre to the next, often taking an examination at one centre in the morning and then another at a different centre in the afternoon. On two occasions I sat an examination in Southend in Essex in the morning and then made the dash to central London to sit an examination there for another board. By the end of the examination assault I was completely exhausted, but happy that I had given them my best shot. It was now a case of waiting for the results to arrive in about eight weeks' time.

I then waited for the twelve examination results for the four subjects to come in. The wait seemed to go on forever, and as time passed my confidence gradually dissipated. Then the results began to arrive, a separate envelope for each subject in my case. In the beginning I couldn't bear to open them and Olivia had to take the plunge. I was astounded to find that I had passed one after the other, and by the time the last results came in I couldn't tear the envelopes open quick enough to confirm every single exam had been a success, and with good grades. This gave me my first insight that I might have some latent talent that had been stunted at the time of the unfortunate Eleven-Plus experience so many years before. At twenty-seven years of age it seemed I might be at the beginning of an academic career.

I was later to successfully add several more subjects to my haul at both "O" level and also "A" level, but in the meantime I decided to apply for entry into teacher training. The entry requirement was five "O" levels, and I only had four. My aim was to obtain the offer of a place for the following year of entry, when I would hopefully have obtained the necessary minimum requirements. Success in this application would motivate me to obtain the last examination I needed.

Although I was fully aware that I could not fulfil the entry requirements for teacher training, I thought I would apply anyway for the experience of filling in the application form. The form did give me a bit of a giggle at one point where it asked me to state, "The place where you studied for your examinations?" I answered truthfully, "On the train between Benfleet Station in Essex and Fenchurch Street Station in London." Perhaps the person reading my application was amused or intrigued by my answer because I was granted an interview.

On the day I was to attend my interview at North East London Polytechnic, everything went wrong. The weather was atrocious with thick snow and freezing fog. Public transport was in complete disarray. I was late at the railway station, the train was late, and it was obvious that I was going to be very late for my interview. I thought to myself, "There's no point in going on to the interview, I'm too late, I don't have the entry requirements. I might as well go home." But the thought of going home and telling my wife I had ducked out made me go on, even though I was going to be very late through no fault of my own.

I arrived at the college and reported to the secretary of the academic who was to interview me. Before I could offer an apology and an explanation for my late arrival, she apologised, saying to me that, unfortunately, my interviewer had 'phoned in to say he would be late due to the bad weather. I was asked to sit and wait. The interview was now two hours behind time, but I had only just arrived anyway.

I had only been waiting for a very few minutes when the interviewer arrived, clearly very flustered. I was ushered into his office and, again, before I could say a word, he was profusely apologising for keeping me waiting for two hours. I certainly wasn't going to enlighten him of his mistake.

I felt that, inadvertently, I had gained a distinct advantage in this interview and my confidence rose. I was offered a place on the next cohort of trainee teachers, instead of waiting for another year, on the proviso that I obtained the further "O" level I needed. This was all the motivation I needed, and suddenly what had started as a seemingly disastrous day became one of success.

To obtain the final "O" level I needed I enrolled in an evening class for art, for which I already had some talent, and taught myself British Constitution for good measure. Later I took "self taught" "A" level Economics and "A" level British Constitution. This learning bug was really taking a hold on my life.

Eventually I joined my course, financed by a meagre but welcome education grant. The financial hardship for me and my family was to continue, but I continued to supplement my grant with judo activities, particularly in youth centres. I also undertook any part-time work I could at weekends and during holiday periods. By this time my wife was also helping in a youth centre as an assistant to the warden. This all helped out financially, and we were even able to afford modest camping holidays for our family.

I was obviously delighted to take up the place on the teacher-training course, and the provision of a grant, modest though it was, pleased me in many ways. It did seem wonderful that the government was not only paying the fees for my course, but also going a long way towards supporting my family while I was improving my personal development.

Receiving the finance I was given did give rise to some personal inner conflict with principles my father had instilled in me. My father did not believe in luck, and neither did I. Any gain to be made from life had to be earned through hard work, and you were not to expect to get anything for nothing. To invest in the stock market was immoral, as was any form of gambling. I had drawn unemployment benefit, and now I was receiving a government grant that would give me personal benefit. However, these regrets did not last long.

As one might expect, most of the other students on the course were much younger than myself, but I, and the other couple of "wrinklies", got on well with the youngsters and they were very helpful to those of us who were new to studying.

I didn't look on my course as being a cause for trepidation. I considered I was being given a wonderful new start in life. I avidly absorbed all the new learning that was on offer. I was like someone who had been starved for a long time, and then sat in front of a feast.

My first two weeks at the teacher training college were a whirl of confusion. I dashed from one place to another, trying to familiarise myself with all the rooms I had to attend, and when I needed to be there.

Olivia and I realised that things were going to be even tighter financially than ever before over the next few years while I was doing teacher-training. We decided to sell our half-decent family car and buy a cheaper one.

When we went to buy an "old banger" to see us through, the salesman said we would get a lot of pleasure out of it. He was right. It was a pleasure to get out of. It developed one problem after another. On one occasion I took it to a garage for repairs and the mechanic suggested we should pray for it to get better. But it never did.

We called this car Gladys, although there was little to be glad about it. We would bowl along in Gladys, my foot down to the floorboards, pushing the old girl up to forty miles an hour, if we were on the straight and had the wind behind us.

One day I was going down a slight hill with a tailwind and reached forty-three miles an hour, an unheard of achievement. We were waved into a lay-by at the bottom of the hill by a policeman on a motor cycle. The officer gave me a friendly warning about breaking the forty mile an hour speed limit. He asked if I had been observing the speedometer. I said that when getting to such giddy speeds it was necessary to concentrate solely on the driving in Gladys. He even smiled when I assured him that I didn't realise the old girl was capable of reaching the speed limit, let alone exceeding it.

For Gladys this was a bit like breaking the sound barrier and I couldn't help feeling a sense of achievement for her. The policeman let me off with a friendly warning. Fortunately he didn't notice that the driver's seat was balanced on a wooden box. I'm sure that today the road police would be much more severe in their dealing with such precarious seating. On another occasion the box was to cause Gladys an indignant injury to her rear end when the seat slid off the box during one of Olivia's excursions in her.

Soon after this incident we sold Gladys for £50. The guy who bought her gave me £20 deposit and promised to bring the remainder when he got paid. He never did pay the balance, but I still think he got the worst of the bargain. I next bought a small second-hand automatic motor scooter (a Triumph Tina) to use for the journey to the railway station. This cost me the princely sum of £5.

There was not a lot of power in the engine, firstly, because the engine was small and, secondly, it was very ancient. When I bought the scooter it had a very good windscreen that protected me while driving along. However, on a windy day the engine didn't have enough power to cope safely with the wind resistance. And when large lorries drove past I had to fight like mad to stop the whole outfit, me included, being swept into the ditch alongside the road. So, the windscreen had to come off, and I faced the elements bravely.

I began a habit of starting the scooter up on its stand in the morning, and leaving it to warm up in preparation for the journey to the railway station. While it was ticking over, I would pop back into the house for a last cup of tea. One day, while Olivia and I were having this last minute cuppa, we saw the scooter begin to move past the window. Somehow, it had put itself into drive and it was moving off, still supported by its stand. We dashed out to find it on its side revving like mad against our garage wall. It only ever did this once but the incident seemed to add to its character. The scooter served me through all weather conditions and at the end of my college days I sold it on for £5 — exactly the price I had paid for it. This was one of my better "deals"!

I was part of a cohort of more than fifty student teachers. These were divided between those who intended to become teachers in junior schools and those, like me, who were destined for secondary schools. Each was sub-divided into areas of subject specialities.

The specialist sub-group I elected to join was for business education, which seemed most appropriate considering the business experience I had had. My group consisted of six male students. Three of our group were mature students and the others were teenagers much younger than us. They were straight from sixth form colleges, and had just completed "A" level studies. In this respect the younger members of

196

the group were better qualified than the other mature students and me, and we were far removed from the rigours of tutored studying. However, these young people were very supportive of us "wrinklies" and they gave us a lot of valuable help and guidance during our early weeks of studying at this high and intense level.

The format of the studies for the full cohort was broken into three broad areas: the theory of education, including psychology, philosophy and teaching pedagogy; general education, which were short courses in the full range of school subjects, including English, mathematics, science, music, art, physical education; and also, specialist studies, which in my case was business education, comprising economics, commerce, economic history, and other business-related areas.

The whole cohort attended large lectures on the theory of education. I found these group sessions to be too large and impersonal and gained only limited use from them. Twice a week we also attended lectures in smaller groups with our personal tutor. I found these latter sessions more constructive, and offering greater opportunity for questions and discussions. It was in these smaller sessions that the first spark of my interest in psychology was to emerge.

I was set my first assignment and given a reading list of nine books by my tutor. This was the first time I had been given a list of reference books. I was required to present the essay in two weeks' time. I knew I could not possibly read nine books in two weeks, on top of the reading lists I was being given for other assignments, and I told my tutor so. "Good God, Alan", he said, "you are not supposed to read them all, just take the bits you need." Realising I had made a bit of a fool of myself, I hardly dared to ask how you find the bits you need. But I desperately needed more information, and continued on with the persistence of a double-decker bus trying to fly. "How long does the essay have to be?" I stammered. "How long is a piece of string", came the terse reply. "Look, Alan, you make it as long as it needs to be. I don't want any waffle, just the guts of the thing. You could do it in half a dozen pages. But if you have nothing to say you could stretch it to a dozen." Later I was to realise that this statement was invaluable, although at the time it just added to my confusion.

I dashed off to the library straightaway, but only to find that just four books were available. Many of the students had of course been given the same assignment by their tutors and they had already visited the library and ransacked it before I got there.

I went to see the group of young friends I had made and told them my tale of woe. They were sympathetic and helpful. For a start they showed me that between us we had all of the reference books we needed, and I had obtained more books than them anyway — they didn't even try to get them all. The sharing round of the books was the obvious answer to that part of my problem.

They also showed me how to use the index at the back of the book to locate the possible areas of interest, and how to quickly discard sections irrelevant to the assignment. They gave me my first lessons in speed reading which I was later to develop extremely well.

They even discussed the structure of the essay with me. When I asked if this wasn't cheating they found it amusing. I will always be grateful to those young lads for the help and guidance they gave me at this crucial stage in my academic development.

My first essay came back with masses of red scribble on it that gave the impression of a spider bleeding to death. I had an instant rapport with it — the spider that is. In spite of the many red notations, the feedback was constructive if not encouraging, and I was sure I could go forward and improve on my work, especially with the help of my new found young friends.

During the breaks between college terms I did a variety of part-time jobs to help make ends meet. One of the occasional jobs I took on was mail-sorting at the main Post Office. In spite of the early morning start this could be a source of good fun. The collection of undeliverable items would alone be an excellent basis of a book. So, any "Posties" out there, get writing!

The main reason for items being undeliverable was the inadequacy of the address. Typical were postcards written to "Rose and Reg of Canvey Island — sorry we've forgotten your address." But even official letters were not beyond reproof. One sorter asked me how they were supposed to deliver an "IMPORTANT NOTICE", to someone of "No fixed abode"?

To supplement our studies of English economic history, a group of us trainee teachers organised a week's holiday on a canal barge. There were ten of us in all. We took turns at cooking our communal meal, and also with the chores of keeping the barge clean and tidy.

199

The tranquillity of slowly following a route where the sound of road traffic was rarely heard is difficult to convey. There was a sense of going back to a bygone age. Negotiating locks became an exciting diversion from our slow progress. This was truly the best way to learn about the golden age of canal transport. Visiting canal-side pubs became an important pastime, and these were incorporated into our schedule for midday and overnight stops. Following one such stop at lunch time resulted in near disaster.

Our canal barge was so long that it took some skilful steering and engine management to negotiate some of the bends in rivers that were incorporated into our route. Unfortunately, we were not that skilful. Consequently, it was not unusual for us to get stuck on a mud-bank. This signalled the need for a couple of us to man a long pole to push, with the engine turning at full power to assist.

On one such "stranding" our boat was firmly embedded into a mud-bank, and no amount of reverse engine thrust could dislodge us. Together with one of the youngest members of the party, Donald, I got the pole and together we worked until our combined pushing and the reverse thrust of the engine freed our bows. The barge now shot away quite lively. Unfortunately, Donald was still attached to the barge pole — which was still stuck firmly in the mud. The sight of Donald slowly sliding down the pole into the water caused the rest of us to collapse with laughter. Fortunately, the water was not too deep and we were able to rescue him, unharmed but smelling dreadfully!

An important aspect of the teacher training course was teaching practice. Each student was allocated to a school for six weeks to practice their teaching techniques under the overall supervision of their personal tutor, but particularly in the care of the class teacher in the allocated school.

I was surprised to be allocated a junior school in Southend for my first practice as I had expected to go to a secondary school: after all, that was where I intended to teach, and that was where my subject specialism lay. But I did not question the placement; ours was to "do and die, not to question why." Two other students were also sent to this school.

We were each placed under the supervision of the teacher of the class we were taking over. All three of us were enthusiastic of having the opportunity to put into practice the ideas we had been working on in college, although I had some apprehension because my preparation had been for much older children.

The lady whose class I was taking over was very supportive and her guidance helped me to grow in confidence. The ten-year-old children in the class had been superbly conditioned by their teacher and only one boy was liable to cause difficulty. The class teacher readily confirmed that he also caused her concern.

As one might expect with this young age group, the things they said and their answers to questions were unpredictable and often amusing. For example, having spent some time talking about hearing, seeing and feeling, I asked the class to name some of the senses. Of all the hands that shot up I chose a boy who could

201

hardly keep his bottom on his chair, so eager was he to share his knowledge. "Common sense and nonsense" was his excited offering.

Periodically our personal tutor would come in unexpectedly to sit in on a lesson or two. This was another opportunity when a child's response to questions would be the cause of amusement, although I sometimes worried needlessly that this would raise questions of my teaching ability. For example, having spent some time talking about Joan of Ark, I threw out what I thought was a simple question. "Who was Joan of Ark?" I asked. I chose an upheld hand at random and back came the reply, "Noah's sister." On another occasion I was seriously informed that the inhabitants of Moscow are called "Mosquitoes". One answer I considered clever was that "a curve is the longest distance between two points."

During the visit of our personal tutor he would discuss our progress with the class teacher and subsequently go through any points made with us and his own observations. The feedback from my class teacher was very positive, but I was very surprised to learn that one of the other students had been slated by his class teacher as completely unsuitable for teaching.

I was surprised by this because as part of the process of the teaching practice we took time to sit in on some of the lessons of each other. My honest view was that this particular student was the best of all three of us, and he was certainly the most suited to the age group of children we were currently involved with.

I made my frank view known to our personal tutor. We concluded that for some reason his class teacher had taken a personal dislike to him, because the tutor could not fault his teaching. The "failing" student was offered the opportunity to carry out another practice in a different school. However, the damage to his self-esteem was so bad that he had a nervous breakdown and ended up in a mental hospital. I went to visit him on several occasions but nothing could bring him back from the depression into which he had sunk. He never rejoined our course and I am convinced that the teaching profession lost a young man who would have proved to be an outstanding teacher of junior age children.

When it came to my second teaching practice I was again placed in a junior school. I grumbled quite a bit about the placement, but perhaps not forcibly enough. Armed with the experience I had gone through earlier in the course, I found the teaching practice extremely useful, even though the class teacher was much more demanding than the previous person I had worked with.

At the time of my third and final teaching practice I was allocated yet another junior school. At this rate I thought I might have difficulty obtaining employment in a secondary school, having never taught that age group. This time I decided to dig my heels in and went to confront my tutor with the problem as I saw it.

I was amazed when my tutor expressed surprise at my complaint. He said that he had assumed that I wanted to become a junior teacher. I couldn't understand how anyone could believe that someone specialising in business education could want to teach at junior level, quite apart from the fact that I was in the secondary teachers' cohort. But the satisfactory outcome was that I was placed in a secondary school for my final teaching practice.

The contrast between working in a junior school and a secondary was a shock initially, especially as the students I was now teaching ranged from age fourteen to eighteen, and studying at "O" level and "A" level standard. I was teaching my specialist subjects with which I felt particularly confident. However, I also taught a different group of students each hour, making it very difficult to remember the names of individual students, which was something my college put considerable emphasis on.

It was during this teaching practice that I had the surprise of being touched up on more than one occasion. Some of my classes consisted mainly of girls who were part of a group taking a course in secretarial duties; others were predominantly boys' classes. In one of the teenage girls' classes I was moving between the rows of desks, examining the work they were doing in the manner recommended by my college, when I thought I may have been touched intimately. I dismissed this as a figment of my imagination. By the time it happened a third time I retreated behind the safety of my desk and conducted all their lessons from that position.

For this placement my visiting college tutor was one of my specialist subject lecturers. He questioned why I didn't move around the class more and scoffed at my explanation. However, once he had a "strange experience" with a student's ruler he didn't bring this up any more.

The same tutor sat in on a lesson when I was trying to get a lower ability group to understand the difficult concept of the terms balance of trade and balance of payments. My tutor, recognising the difficulty I was experiencing, decided to take over the class to demonstrate to me how it was done. His level of language was way beyond that of this particular class. He failed miserably and pandemonium began to develop. I was forced to take the class back from him in order to restore order. I knew at that moment there was no way I could fail this final teaching practice and my tutor didn't bother to visit again.

At the end of my first year of study I was interviewed by my tutor prior to the issue of my progress report. He asked me to talk frankly about how I was doing on the course, including the "lows" as well as the "highs", and to outline any self doubts I had, so that he could plan to support me. I was surprised to read my own words in my official end of year review. I guessed that my tutor didn't have the ability I had given him credit for, and I felt that I had been cheated.

When I reached the end of the second year, the process was repeated. On this occasion I told my tutor nothing negative about myself but emphasised only my successes. My end of year report read — "Alan has made excellent progress and shows strong confidence in his further development." Since this time I have been very wary of giving so-called "experts" too much credit, and I also try to avoid doing other people's jobs for them.

Towards the end of each academic year, examinations took place. For me it involved taking fourteen three-hour papers. These rapidly followed one after the other over seven days, darting from one subject to another. I had worked hard throughout the year but still had my doubts overhung from the Eleven-Plus experience. However, failure was not an option for me. My whole future depended on my making a success of this new development in my life.

My main weakness as I saw it lay with philosophy. I never really got to grips with the philosophy aspects of my course. It seemed to me to be continually asking vague questions and never providing concrete answers. I might just as well have been asked, "Who killed Cock Robin?" for all the sense I got out of it. However, I passed all the exams, not with any great distinction, but safely, and this left me satisfied. I found the psychology papers particularly interesting, which was not surprising as it was one of my favourite areas of study.

Following the examinations at the end of the third and final year of teacher training, a small group were selected to continue to a fourth year to convert their Teaching Certificate into a bachelor's degree. At this time teachers holding a degree were in the minority, and I desperately wanted to gain a degree, mainly to have "letters after my name". But it was not to be. My personal tutor interviewed me and more or less told me that I did not have what it takes to take my learning to degree level. I hoped to prove him wrong at some time in the future, but I had no idea how.

I felt that my teacher training had been thorough, despite not being given the opportunity to continue my studies to degree level. But I had two particular criticisms of the course. First was the fact that, although dates were set for submission of assessment work, many students did not adhere to these. Consequently, feedback of the correct structure of the "answers" was given by tutors before some students had submitted their work. I viewed this as giving some lax students an unfair advantage.

My second criticism was related to the examinations. Two of the students in my cohort failed to actually sit the final examinations due to "stress". They were granted a pass on the course on the basis of their course work over the three years of the course. I had no argument with this. But I did object to the fact that another student, whose work was satisfactory throughout the course, was failed solely on the basis of the final examination.

Many years later I became the external examiner for the same institution where I trained to become a teacher, and I took great care to ensure that this did not occur during my period of supervision. By the time I was carrying out this office I was the holder of a Ph.D., and immediately within my remit came the work of my former tutor who had told me that I wasn't good enough to do a first degree. This was a very satisfying situation.

Looking back at my three years at teacher-training college, I realise that in many ways it was a turning point in my life: not only from the point of view of my academic improvement, although that was important, but it also helped my personal development. I really matured during this time. I enjoyed my intellectual growth, I also enjoyed being a husband and a father and all the responsibility that went with it. But perhaps most of all, I was getting a lot of satisfaction out of what I saw as a new start in life, and an increase in my self-esteem.

My first teaching appointment took place under strange circumstances. I saw a job advertised for a Head of Department for Commerce at a local grammar school that was in the process of changing to a comprehensive school. Applications were invited in writing. Commerce was one of my specialist subjects at my teacher-training college. Although I knew that a probationary teacher could not be made a head of department, I decided to apply. In my letter, I proposed that I do the job of head of department on the basic pay of a probationer, on the understanding that if I was successful I would be made head of department at the end of the probationary year. If I were not successful I would resign, leaving the school free to appoint a replacement.

My audacious letter must have appealed to the headmaster because I was summoned to an interview and appointed to the school on the terms I had proposed. Once the college term had ended I occasionally visited my new school to familiarise myself with my new appointment, and the rooms and staff I was going to be responsible for.

I went into the lessons of some of my colleagues. I was a little surprised at the number of typewriting classes that the department dealt with, and how few boys were taught by the people who were to be my colleagues. But I liked the style of economics that was being taught.

During one such visit to the school, the departing head of department asked me what typewriting books I would like her to buy on my behalf from the funds allocated to the department for this purpose. I told her I knew nothing about typewriting and she should purchase what she thought was appropriate.

A few days after this brief exchange, I was asked by the headmaster if I could call and see him for a chat. When I arrived he explained that he had been surprised to be told that I knew nothing about typewriting and yet this was the subject for which he had invited applications. I explained that his idea of commerce was very different from mine. I offered to release the school of any obligation to my appointment. However, he invited me to explain how I saw the format of a commerce department. Once he understood my wider vision of the department, and the true description of the subject commerce as descriptive economics, rather than shorthand and typing, he became very enthusiastic to develop the department along these lines, and I remained at this Essex school for twenty-seven years.

CHAPTER
NINE

SCHOOL REPORT

As I had anticipated from my earlier work with youngsters in youth centres, I got along well with young people in the school situation. I enjoyed being a teacher, working with them, and I experienced no discipline problems, but I had considerable apprehension in case disaster would descend upon me.

In fact, disaster did strike during my very first term as an Essex teacher. On the day before the school broke up for the Christmas holidays, I decided I would set my class of teenagers a test to assess how much they had retained from the term's study of an examination subject.

I, naively, thought the class would be delighted at my dedication, and my willingness to give up part of my Christmas holiday to assess their progress. Fool that I was! They were disgruntled at being faced with a test when they were already into "holiday mode". They went on strike and refused to do the test. Talk about "goodwill to all mankind"! It was very tricky biting the bullet and recognising the strategic error of judgement I had made, and then to back down without losing too much face. As it happened, my relationship with this particular class turned out to be one of the best throughout my teaching career.

For most of my early teaching career my main work involved teaching business-related subjects (business studies, economics and office practice) to fourteen to sixteen-year-olds. I was also a form tutor to younger children (aged eleven to thirteen), so I was familiar with the full age range of secondary education. The younger age group could be a source of considerable amusement, especially when observing their misquotes.

I once asked an exuberant boy to give me a sentence with the word "canal" in it. His response was, "at three forty-five, when the bell goes, we canal go home". On another occasion I read where a pupil assured me that Glasgow had "a depraved inner-city area". On another occasion I was teaching a young class when I heard a girl exclaim, "F**k it". I told her sternly that she shouldn't use such bad language. "It's not bad," she said, "It's just what my dad says when the car won't start." One day I was exploring shapes with a young class. "I have three sides and three corners. What am I?" I asked. "Lost", came the quick-fire reply.

One of the rules that politicians, in their wisdom, decided to introduce into the schools' curriculum was a spoonful a day of religion, or something akin to it. What they failed to recognise was that the one thing teachers could refuse to teach was religion. So schools now had a requirement the politicians had introduced, but insufficient staff willing to implement it.

It was not possible to meet the requirement by making every child attend an assembly every day, taken by those willing to implement the requirement, because the largest schools (e.g. secondary schools) could not accommodate all of their pupils in a single assembly hall, assuming that the full age range would benefit from this. And so all sorts of watered down versions of the requirement were devised. In the school where I taught, and many others, we created a daily session called "thought for the day". During the session each form tutor would address some form of moral issue that would not conflict with their religious views. Generally speaking, this worked very well, although there were times when such sessions did not go to plan.

One morning I was taking my young tutor group on "thought for the day". On this particular day we were examining the issues of quarrels, and I had emphasised that you cannot have a quarrel unless two people are involved. I chose a rather forward girl to stand up and complete a sentence I had written on the blackboard: "It takes two to make . . . " (I was looking for the answer, "a quarrel"). "Love" was the brazen response, to which some of the class of eleven year olds tittered, but the majority of them looked on bemused in their innocence.

Sometimes the pupils themselves chose the topics they wanted to discuss during these sessions. An issue that I found worried many young pupils was cancer. I surveyed one class and found that there were only a few that had not experienced the loss of someone close to them through cancer. But they were confused at the variety of forms that cancer takes. We spent a long time exploring the issue and some really mature written work came out of it, but it also gave some amusing contributions. For example, I set the innocuous question, "What do we mean by the word benign?" and received one response of, "We benign after we be eight."

Taking "thought for the day" lessons was very much like "live" television. You ask a question and then choose one of many raised hands to give a response. You never know what the chosen youngster might say, but whatever is offered, no matter how wildly incorrect, it is always important not to show any derision. During one "thought for the day" lesson a boy insisted that Jesus' father painted cars. When I asked where he got this idea from he asserted, "Well my mum said he was a car painter, and I believe my mum". Very wise to believe one's mum!

The written work of youngsters also contains much humour. I used the tutor period to get young pupils to write about their personal experiences, drawing on what had taken place during the past week. This not only encouraged them to write creatively, but it also gave me some insight into their home background. The work was sent home so that parents could read what they had written.

One child wrote, "My dad's working away this week. So my mum is sleeping with Fred again." The next day after the work had gone home to the parents to read, I received a terse note from mum. "Dear Teacher, I would like to point out that Fred is our dog."

Another parent came to see me once. She had been reading her daughter's "news" writing, and wanted to assure me that some of the things she had written were not as accurate as they appeared. To relieve her embarrassment I told her, "If you promise not to believe everything she says happens at school, I promise not to believe everything she says happens at home."

On another occasion I once set my young tutor group a simple piece of homework, in which I asked them to give a brief description of the entrance to their house in no more than twenty words. Rebecca wrote, "There is a lot of rough mating in the hall."

While doing their creative writing, I encouraged the children to tell me words they were not sure how to spell. If they were words I felt they should be able to look up in the dictionary I would point them in this direction, but if the word was more ambiguous (as so many English words can be), I would write it on the blackboard. One boy asked, "How do you write fought, Sir?" "Do you mean, like, the two men fought, or the fort where soldiers live?" I asked. "No, I mean the fought you fink in yer ed", came the exasperated reply.

Another teacher told me she was asked how to spell "potato clock". She had never heard of this, but, assuming it was some new-fangled trend for clocks, she wrote it on the board. Later, at break time, she asked around the staff room whether any one had heard of this newest craze, but no one else knew of it. Then later that day she read the lad's work — "Every morning I get up potato clock."

On another occasion I had long discussions with a class about the effects of an oil tanker that had run aground on the rocks, and the effects the pollution was

214

having on the shore. This incident was receiving a lot of media coverage at the time. I asked the class to write about the effects of oil on fish. One child wrote, "My mum opened a tin of sardines last night. It was full of oil and all the fish were dead."

When discussing this funny response with a science teacher, she told me about an answer she had received when she had asked, "What is cross-pollination?" One of the rather forward girls in her class had written, "It's when a female flower is not in the mood."

One day I found an exercise book in the school corridor. As I thought I knew the name on the book I stopped the boy to return it. "It's not mine," he said, "It's my brother's; he's in the next form. He's six months older than me." Before I could recover from this remark of brothers with only six months gap between them, the boy went on. "One of us is adopted, but I can't remember which." The words lifted my spirits, trying to visualise the home where being adopted makes so little difference.

When I was at school my school reports used to be given to me in a brown sealed envelope. I would take them home in trepidation, as my parents attached considerable importance to my standing in school. Generally speaking my reports were fair and accurate, but sometimes they contained cryptic messages with elements of truth, for example, "Always first with the answer, but not always correct," or, "If he would think more carefully before he speaks he would do better."

I'm sure that many of today's parents do not realise the volume of work that is put into report writing by teachers, in order to make them worthwhile, truthful and accurate. Teachers write their report of a child trying to succinctly and accurately summarise a whole year of study, work and assessment. The report is then passed to another more senior colleague to check, and then to another for a further check. At each stage, when errors or disparities are noticed, the report will be returned to the author for rewriting.

While reading and checking the reports of other teachers many amusing comments could be seen. The following are some I noted down at the time and saved for posterity:

> Damian is trying — very trying.
> John's writing has now improved sufficiently, so that now it is possible to recognise just how bad his work is.
> Lucy's mind is full of information, but this is only of interest to herself.

There are also lots of clichés which occur frequently in reports that contain a hidden meaning:

> Communicates fluently — doesn't stop talking.
> A natural leader — a right bossy boots.
> Is an independent learner — refuses to do as he is told.
> Needs to try harder — bone idle.

It can be tricky when the teacher needs to write to the parent. It is necessary to make them aware of the reason for the letters without offending or alienating them. But often the facts of the circumstance make tact difficult, and sometimes the response from the parent is not what was hoped.

I once had the difficult situation in that a child was being shunned in class because her personal hygiene left a lot to be desired. So I wrote what I considered to be a tactful letter suggesting that the mother could encourage the girl to have regular showers or baths, and frequent changes of clothes. Back came the blunt reply: "Dear Teacher, I don't see no problem. Your job is to teach, not to smell." I was obviously not as tactful as I intended, or perhaps I was too tactful!

It was about this time in my teaching career that there was a big push by the government to encourage people to "Embrace Europe", and teachers were encouraged to promote healthy debate with pupils, but I had doubts about the sincerity of the politicians who were hell bent on taking us down this road.

I have lots of friends in other European countries and I have a lot of affection for them. In particular I have close friends in Germany and Spain and they have helped me to embrace the idea of being a "European" as well as being British, although I found it difficult to equate the whole development with my other friends in the Commonwealth. Where did it leave our relationship with them, I questioned?

In spite of some misgivings, my initial reaction to Britain joining the "Common Market" was reasonably enthusiastic, although this was tempered by a feeling that in doing so we were betraying our long-standing

217

trading partners in the Commonwealth. I remember, when I was a seaman, visiting a port in one of our colonies and seeing an amusing bit of graffiti that said — "British go home, but please take me with you." So, some saw the value of being British, and was there a case for us to remain independent from the rest of Europe? However, many of our former colonies clearly wanted to loosen their links with Britain, so it made sense that it was time for us to move on also.

Surely joining the European Economic Community was the right direction to follow? Increased prosperity, friendliness and relatively free trade between the nations of Europe would be good for all the member countries, without incurring foreign interference in domestic political matters. I was sold on the idea eventually and, like most teachers at that time, I meekly followed the directions of the government and did my best to encourage my pupils to "Embrace Europe", even though it seemed that the population as a whole were divided on the issue.

What I, and so many others failed to take into account was the separate personal agenda some of our political masters were intent on following, irrespective of the views of the people who gave them their positions of representation. We only slowly became aware of the real intent to build a European super-state, for so good was the brainwashing and mass hypnotism. But to express alarm at the way the politicians are running out of control in building their own personal "gravy train" today results in being branded a "Euro-sceptic", or even ill-informed. Dissidents are to be disowned as "anti-Europe", even if they possess high regard for other countries.

Out of this, the myth has been created that many Britons are anti-Europe, rather than acknowledge their simple desire to maintain their national identity which is being threatened and perverted by those with a vested interest in a European super-state. Unfortunately, I feel I played my part in encouraging my pupils to embrace a new Europe, and today I have doubts that I was right to do so.

One of the most satisfying education curriculum developments that I was personally involved in creating was a collection of courses for the very low ability older student (e.g. fourteen- to sixteen-year-olds). These pupils were those who could not cope with taking formal examinations across the full range of the curriculum.

For these pupils I designed a collection of courses in modular format. The subject matter was such that they could see the relevance of it to their adult life. Areas of learning included life skills topics such as operating a bank account, saving, investing and borrowing, consumer protection, and similar topics — even planning a holiday. Filling out forms, to obtain a passport or a driving licence etc, were warmly received because they saw the future use of this experience.

The main philosophy of the courses was to more or less guarantee the students were going to be successful, no matter how weak their level of ability was. The emphasis was on willing participation and cooperation rather than level of performance. This was to be important because in so many more formal subjects they were failing and disruptive.

As previously mentioned, the courses were divided into modules, with each module assessed by the teacher. The aim was to give positive reinforcement at every opportunity. Negative reinforcement was avoided like the plague! Each module resulted in a school certificate that was as elaborately printed as any of the formal examinations, and the certificate was individually signed by the head-teacher and the class teacher responsible for the module assessment.

The pupils taking these courses were often disruptive in other lessons because they were not experiencing success, no matter how hard they tried. So, they gave up trying. But their enthusiasm for the special non-examination courses did lead to some tricky situations.

To dissuade one particular group from swearing, I introduced a swear box. The box was monitored by the youngsters themselves. By a few weeks before Christmas they had amassed quite a haul of money. I suggested that I should take the money and buy a load of sweets that could be shared out on the last day of term. It was explained to me, very pleasantly, that it was their money and they had their own ideas for its use. Democracy ruled and I, foolishly, insisted they tell me how it would be used.

The class had decided they would put the money down as a bet on a horse. I argued that I had never been in a betting shop in my life, and that I could not play any part in such a venture. However, I was assured

220

that, "Stuart's dad was willing to place the bet on their behalf."

What then ensued was three weeks of solid maths, where they spent lesson after lesson, teaching their apparently "stoopid" teacher how odds and winnings were calculated. They also demonstrated, mathematically, how they would choose a suitable nag to put the money on. In effect, I got three weeks of maths out of them through pure trickery, while they were an absolute pain for their normal maths teacher.

My constructive delaying tactics took us nicely up to the Christmas break. I passed over the money and left their fate in the hands of Stuart's dad. I did worry during the holiday period that I might read a newspaper headline revealing, "School pupils win a fortune from a swear box." But my fears were unfounded. They lost the lot!

These low ability pupils responded well to these courses simply because they saw the relevance of them, and found they were experiencing success. Unfortunately, the courses were forced out of the curriculum by a management team that saw league tables and formal exams as more important than what was proving successful with youngsters who were disillusioned with much of the education they were struggling with. Not surprisingly, following the movement away from this type of course, and the eventual imposition of the National Curriculum, we saw the increase in disruption in classrooms.

I found that I got along well with other teachers and for the greater part I found them dedicated colleagues,

221

who often gave much more to their pupils than some of them deserved. Working hours remained an "open cheque book" throughout my teaching career of thirty years. Teachers always seemed willing to cast aside their own rights and entitlements and work undefined hours at the whim of their employers. They were continually asked to embrace new working practices and rarely received the reward they deserved for the changes they were required to implement.

The Essex school where I spent most of my teaching career employed some sixty-five highly qualified staff. With such a large number of intelligent professional people, and a wide variety of personalities, one soon learnt the need to think before you put your mouth into gear. This was particularly so in large meetings where there was always someone who would pounce on a carelessly worded phrase and expose its flaws.

Although this may sound as if the teachers that one addressed at meetings were petty nit-pickers, this was not the case. In teaching, colleagues were far more demanding, and sometimes more cleverly devious, than those I had experienced in business. They kept you on your toes and it was a most rewarding learning curve to be on.

Probably one of the most significant learning experiences I have gained has come from exchanges with women teachers. They were quick to point out where something I said could be interpreted as a sexist comment. I quickly learnt to recognise ahead when wording I was about to use could be misinterpreted, and I benefited from this knowledge in my relationships with others.

Some of my male senior colleagues were slow to learn the feminist strategies, and these astute ladies would verbally rip them apart. One such colleague, who probably thought that "chivalry" meant when you are feeling cold, put his foot in it during a debate and didn't know when to shut up.

His aim was to discourage women teachers from wearing leggings to work. As far as I am concerned, we men are in no-man's land when it comes to discussing women's clothing. It is a definite no-go area for any male discussion. But this guy didn't know when to stop, and he dug himself a hole so deep that a few bright ladies buried him alive. And he deserved it.

Kim was a lady with whom I had a lovely platonic relationship when we worked together as teachers. She was a fierce feminist, and very bright. She regularly chewed up men and spat them out. We got on well together. She tolerated no bull, and I never tried to give her any.

Kim frequently phoned me late at night while my wife and I were in bed. My wife knew Kim also, and didn't mind these late night chats, and Kim and I would talk over professional matters until the early hours, long after my wife had gone to sleep.

One day it was my turn to be on the end of a tongue-lashing from Kim in a large meeting. But I had the last laugh when I suddenly said, "I was lying in bed talking to Kim the other night . . ." The sudden

223

stunned silence in that room was delicious, and Kim took it all in good spirit.

Learning to think ahead became useful in the cut and thrust of smaller, high-powered meetings, when there was often a hidden agenda, and when only too often someone was present who only wanted to score points over others. During such exchanges I developed a style that often disarmed my opponents in debates. One colleague complimented me following such an exchange by saying, "You sliced him up so politely, he didn't even know he was bleeding until it was too late."

All teachers are required to periodically attend courses to update their skills and knowledge. I attended a residential course that aimed to improve listening and communication skills. As part of the course we were paired with another, one male with one female. We were sent out, at night, to visit a local pub. On arriving at our allocated pub we were required to engage complete strangers in conversation. Later we were required to write up an analysis of our experience in terms of the reaction of our victims to the invasion of their space. I was paired with a nun, who was a teacher.

Not surprisingly, this was the first time I had been to a pub with a nun. But Sister Emma had a really good sense of humour, and the experience was good fun. I enjoyed walking up to the bar and asking for, "A pint of bitter for me, and a glass of lemonade for my friend." The barman's face was a picture. Even more amusing was the look on the faces of the very young couple whose space we chose to invade. I've often wondered if their parents believed them later that night when they related who they had been drinking with in the pub earlier in the evening.

The in-service course that was the most effective for me was to last for five years. The then Conservative government introduced the Technical and Vocational Education Initiative (TVEI). The general aim of the initiative was to make the curriculum of secondary schools more relevant to the world of work, and more receptive to the technological developments taking place (particularly the computer-related changes).

Schools have been notoriously reluctant to change, and for a very long time their curriculum had been dominated by an examination system largely controlled by the universities. The TVEI initiative was funded by the then Department of Trade and Industry (DTI) rather than the Department of Education and Science (DES). In this way new money was being offered for effective curriculum change. The money on offer was very substantial and, for the cash-starved schools, proved to be an effective carrot to bring change about.

I was chosen to head up this development in my Essex school and, because my wages and the changes I was intended to initiate were funded separately from the normal DES funding, it gave me a considerable degree of independence from the normal education regime. The whole process was based on a kind of "payment by results" basis, consequently the scheme was almost assured of success. This was one of the few examples I can clearly identify from my teaching career where the government put its money where its mouth was in regard to educational change, and consequently it was more or less assured of success.

Within the overall programme of curriculum change there was an extensive in-service education course, much of which was directed at people in my position of heading up the initiative. The in-service training was some of the best I experienced throughout my teaching career. There were continuous one day weekly courses throughout the whole five years of the initiative. These focused on areas such as team-building and motivation of staff, which I was then to apply in the work situation. Some of the techniques recommended to encourage teachers were pretty obvious, and common in business, but sadly missing in education. Not surprisingly, teachers responded well to being treated well and respected, but throughout the programme some senior managers could never fully take on board the new approach to people management that the initiative tried to promote.

The reason why some management teams seemed unwilling to accept the TVEI initiative, may have been the fact that one of the aims of it was to encourage autonomy of teachers; to give them a sense of ownership of the new development. I suspect that some senior managers felt threatened by the independence that teachers were being encouraged to adopt.

Sadly, although this initiative was well-founded and effective, during the last year of its operation, the same government that had implemented it effectively killed it off with the implementation of the National Curriculum. Whereas TVEI had encouraged free thinking

226

and versatile curriculum development, it seemed that, at the time, the implementation of the National Curriculum had the reverse effect.

The curriculum was now placed in a straight jacket more restricting than ever before. Many initiatives at the school level were destroyed. Pupils had less choice of what they would learn during their last two years of their secondary education, and consequently seemed less motivated at this important stage of their academic and personal development. Perhaps not surprisingly, pupil behaviour in schools began to worsen.

Many teachers were not happy with the introduction of the National Curriculum either. They felt that something was being "done to them", and had no confidence that the philosophy of the change had been thoroughly thought through. The government went through the theoretical process of consulting the teachers who were required to deliver the new procedures, but the teachers felt that in reality little consideration was given to their suggestions. Here was yet another example of politicians changing direction, without the foresight and consultation that is needed, just as they so often do.

Sadly, many of the teaching senior managers of schools I worked with seemed to readily forget the circumstances they had experienced in full classroom teaching once they were promoted. And yet they had experienced the real world of the chalk face at some time in their career. They should have had some sympathy with their non-management colleagues, but

227

too often it seemed they readily betrayed former colleagues.

When I eventually became a senior manager of a school, it seemed to me that there was a collective conspiracy of some managers to deny teachers lower down in the hierarchy the recognition of the dedicated work they do. Perhaps I was unfortunate to experience some managers lacking in foresight, although a similar view was often conveyed to me by teachers in other schools, so it does seem that this may have been a malady in teaching generally.

In spite of my disappointment with some of the senior managers I worked with, my thirty years as a teacher were immensely satisfying. I particularly enjoyed the later years as a senior manager when I was involved in the career development of teachers. During this time in my teaching career my knowledge of people management was on a steady upward learning curve. I found teachers responded positively to the changes and improvements they were required to implement if they were approached in the right manner, and if their views and concerns were acknowledged.

One of the roles I carried out as a senior manager at a large comprehensive school was that of staff induction advisor. This involved acting as a mentor to all new members of staff, whether they were newly qualified teachers (NQTs) or experienced teachers. This included observation in the classroom and then offering guidance for professional development. Such observations had their amusing incidences. Once I was observing a home economics teacher demonstrating

228

making an apple crumble. The teacher said to the class, "Cut the apples carefully and don't waste anything. They don't grow on trees you know." And reading one child's notes I chuckled at his heading — "Making Apple Grumble".

Differentiation has always been an important aspect of good teaching technique, but several government initiatives (for example the introduction of the GCSE) gave it increased focus. Recognition of the need to differentiate means considerably more work for the dedicated teacher. It involves identifying the different levels of knowledge and development of each pupil, and the varying learning strategies that work best for them. Based on this knowledge the teacher will structure teaching strategies to the needs of the individual. In other words, several teaching strategies have to be designed for each class. This is very demanding and time-consuming for the teacher, but necessary for the individual development of each pupil.

One NQT that I was supervising was clearly not differentiating in his teaching, and was not responding to the guidance I was offering him. Having tried unsuccessfully to get him to grasp the concept of differentiation, I suggested I would send him on a course. His response was, "I don't need a course. On my teacher training course I was taught to differentiate, and I am always careful to recognise the difference between boys and girls." Needless to say, I insisted that he needed to attend the course, and he did at least learn what differentiation meant.

When I was at school in my youth I respected my teachers, even those I didn't like very much. My parents looked on teaching as a profession that was admired. This attitude towards teachers still existed when I qualified as a teacher. So, I was proud to become a teacher and for at least fifteen years after qualifying I felt this way. I enjoyed working with young people and I found the job very satisfying. I found that all youngsters inspired me, even the so-called "difficult" kids. I did not experience problems and I rarely had a need to punish for misdemeanours.

But then, it seemed to me that the attitude towards teachers began to change. This change was undoubtedly initiated by senior politicians who consistently used teachers as a punchbag, particularly when the teaching profession questioned some of the daft ideas that the politicians and their civil servants cooked up as part of their ill-founded experiments. Most of these were aimed at increasing control over teachers rather than improving the quality of education. And the sincerity of the reasons for changes was thrown into severe doubt by frequent further changes. How a bunch of politicians could come up with some of the crackpot ideas they did was a mystery worthy of Agatha Christie.

If the politicians do not respect the opinions of the highly trained and superbly qualified experts they employ, it is perhaps not surprising that some parents picked up the vibes of the politicians through the parts of the media that supported the government of the day. This in turn was reflected in the attitude of schoolchildren towards education and towards teachers also.

If the ever-changing developments politicians keep coming up with are supposed to be the answers to the questions the "normal" sections of our society keep asking, we must be asking some pretty daft questions. Considering the track record of too many politicians, it is surprising that so much of the media would uncritically promote their often ill-considered ideas, or that the general public could not spot it when they were clearly experimenting with the lives of their children.

After all, these politicians were the people who encouraged the sale of school playing fields (which belonged to the local community and not the schools), at the same time as they were bemoaning the decline of sporting achievement of our young people. And the idea of the sale of playing fields was attractive to some schools because the politicians starved them of cash. These same politicians introduced a National Curriculum that removed most of the initiative from teaching, reduced educational choice, and decided that all children should learn a second language, even if they were struggling with their first. At the same time a blind eye was turned to immigrants who were unwilling to fully learn English. They then introduced testing of children (repeatedly) with tests that the politicians would probably not pass themselves. It was hardly surprising that many children became disaffected with the education they were receiving, and many teachers also despaired of what they were being asked to deliver.

231

And who did our politicians blame? You guessed it — the teachers of course.

Not surprisingly teachers began to leave the profession in their thousands, to pursue more satisfying jobs, or to take early retirement, and a whole generation of highly-experienced educators were lost. And how did these highly paid, part-time politicians try to fill the gap? By expecting prospective teachers to borrow money to pay for their own training, thus saddling themselves with a debt for years to come! And when this didn't work their next solution was to suggest that untrained people such as teaching assistants should be allowed to teach.

Teaching assistants make a valuable contribution to the education of children, but they are not teachers. If they wanted to become teachers they would train to do so. They are paid derisory wages, and for this reason they appeal to the government as a source of cheap labour, which could save paying teachers the level of salary necessary to address the perennial retention crisis.

So it was now clear that the ideology of an all-degree profession could be abandoned, and now it was deemed that anyone could do the job that most responsible parents would trust only the best to do (and certainly not a politician!). Perhaps soon there will be scope for a plumber to become a brain surgeon, and maybe to be allowed to practice on politicians!

Schools became so strapped for cash that raising money privately to keep them going became as important as the education that should have been their sole priority. Applicants for teaching posts began including in their curriculum vitae details of their record for raising money. One began to read of "heroes" who had almost solely replenished a whole library, or had bought a new set of balls for the head of the PE department. Assuming the head of PE is a male!

The irony of all this is that both Conservative and Labour governments have readily funded wars at the stroke of a pen, while in the meantime education and medical care are starved of funds in real terms. We are repeatedly told that we cannot afford to fund state pensions in the long term any more, we cannot afford a welfare state in the manner to which we have been accustomed, and cures for the most prominent illnesses our culture faces rely on research supported by charities. Wouldn't it be good if schools and hospitals had all the staff and equipment they needed, and the army had to hold jumble sales and fun runs to buy weapons?

So, it seems that we can readily find money for weapons (that we hope we will never use) while in the meantime hospitals and schools are starved of cash, we fail to care for the elderly, can't afford to fund a welfare state any more, or support research to develop a cure for cancer. There is no such thing as free university education any more, so we are back to a system of university education for the financially elite who can afford it, or for the poor souls who tie a lifetime of debt around their necks for the privilege of a degree that doesn't guarantee employment anyway.

We had government after government with plenty of ideas and initiatives, but pie in the sky ideas of how they would be financed. The whole country was to become computer literate, spearheaded by education, but largely financed by fundraising. Or perhaps schools could form "partnerships" with benevolent businesses?

Well, businesses pricked up their ears at this idea. Soon parents were being told how much to spend in their local superstore, for which the store would fund the purchase of a few books for the school library. Or they were being extolled to spend a large sum of money in stores, in return for which the shop would provide a single computer to help make the country computer literate.

It didn't take long before schools were being exhorted to replace displays of kids' work in corridors with imposing advertisements extolling some fast food giant. And money-making drinks and snack machines were being installed in school dining rooms to raise extra funds. But, at the same time, schools were being reminded of their responsibility to encourage their pupils to eat healthily!

Raising money for their cash starved schools became a major priority for teachers and school governors. Boot sales, fun runs, quiz nights and raffles were becoming as time-consuming as extra-curricular activities. What should have been happening was that teachers, parents and governors should have been screaming from the roof tops, "What about our youngsters', and the country's, future?" There was some shouting, but most of it was whimpering, with the politicians shouting about how they know what is best.

Acronyms became the "in" thing in education. Everything had to have one, because so many of the titles of the unending initiatives to pour out from the political nest were so long that they became unmanageable as title headings.

The main call to arms for fighting the cash starvation trend was, Save Our Schools (SOS), although perhaps it should have been, Save our Dying Schools (SODS), because it really was "sods law" how schools managed financially. Schools were now funding many things that had previously been firmly in the province of central or local government. Rebuild Our Toilets (ROT) aptly reflects the dire state into which British education had descended.

The politicians, of course, insisted that they were pouring more money into education than ever before, but those at the chalk-face couldn't work out where it was going. Could it be that too much was being pumped into ivory towers, where academics and politicians were being paid to concoct yet more cash-consuming experiments?

In *The Peter Principle* in 1966, Lawrence J. Peter proposed that "if you don't know where you're going, you will probably end up somewhere else." This was certainly the case with British education for decades, where experiment after experiment has been implemented and later abandoned at the whim of politicians and their advisers in ivory towers.

There is a straightforward question our politicians need to answer. How was it that a country such as ours, emerging from the Second World War, financially bankrupt, with many of our young men dead, managed to fund a welfare state that was the envy of the world, set up a range of state owned industries that worked (including an effective transport system), promoted an adequately funded education system that was emulated around the globe and enabled even the poorest to go to university, and yet today, our highly paid politicians cannot adequately fund or accept responsibility for any of these? But it does seem that too many of our politicians are able to dump their long-serving wives to take off with a girl younger than their daughters, and yet still lecture everyone else on moral and family issues.

Teachers are often faced with the accusation that their lives are one big holiday, because of the number of holiday breaks they get. But their accusers have a lack of understanding. They are not faced all day with young shrill voices, a need to be "on stage" and entertaining from the first bell until the last. Not to mention every evening spent marking work, preparing for the next day's lessons, writing assessments and reports, often to the detriment of their own family. Even so-called "break" times are dominated by work, interrupted by squabbles in the playground, and subject to interruptions by pupils or other staff.

I was once asked, "Do you have children?" "About 1,350 at the last count", I replied, and then added, "But I say goodbye to them every day at four o'clock, and try desperately to forget they exist until the next day. But that is very hard to do." Most teachers are too dedicated to forget their pupils when they leave the school to go home, which is why they spend an enormous amount of their personal time reading and marking work, with very little acknowledgement of their efforts. This is why so many teachers refer to their job as "an open cheque book of work".

When I first entered the profession, I truly enjoyed teaching. In fact, for much of my teaching career I was happy and proud to be a teacher. But the job changed gradually at first, but more rapidly as the paper chase got quicker. The introduction of the National Curriculum and the testing of children that followed it was the death knell for teaching as I had known it. The changes had the effect of sweeping away the opportunities to really get to know pupils and to be able to give individual quality time when it was needed. This is so essential for the teenagers with whom I worked, who are struggling with the onset of puberty, but also realising the need to decide realistically what they want to do in the future, and how they can meet the expectations of their parents.

Instead of giving time to these important issues, teaching became dominated with following a curriculum geared towards accountability, assessment and examinations. The many aspects of teaching that provided job satisfaction had been swept away, so it was not surprising that an increasing number of very experienced teachers began to look for ways to abandon a sinking ship. For many of them it came,

237

unfortunately, in the form of physical or mental breakdowns.

I once received a card from a past pupil with the words, "to a teacher who made learning fun". So why has all the fun gone out of teaching and learning today? The answer to this question can be found in one word — politicians. And these amateur administrators do not have to teach, and they most certainly didn't experience the National Curriculum that they believe is so good.

By the time of the implementation of the National Curriculum and testing at the secondary age level, I was well established as an author of academic text books, which I describe in a later chapter. I was also qualified, through my doctorate research, to practice as a psychologist. At the age of fifty-six, I knew this was the time to make a change to do those things I enjoyed. It was time to move on in a different direction, but it was a big step to take, and the move away from a regular income to a situation less secure seemed a big risk.

The final nudge to encourage me to take the steps necessary to realise these new ambitions materialised when it was decided to amalgamate the school where I was employed with another. The rules of the game were that both schools had to be closed. Staff of over fifty-five years of age were offered a redundancy package that included immediate access to an enhanced pension and lump sum. With my pension, my income from writing and my part-time private practice as a psychologist, I would be no worse off financially, but I would choose my hours of employment. For me this was a dream come true, and it didn't take too much thinking about to make the final decision.

CHAPTER
TEN

DOLE TO DOCTORATE

It was during my time employed as a teacher in Essex that I began to realise that my academic development had still only scratched the surface of my full potential. Although I was happy teaching and my department had expanded and developed into a highly successful and versatile part of the school, I still felt I wanted to obtain a degree, especially as some of those who worked in my department held a degree.

I was aware of colleges offering part-time degree courses through evening study, but I was still practising judo several nights a week. This was keeping me very fit, and I was becoming close to obtaining the coveted black belt. So I looked for alternative ways of obtaining a degree. The ideal answer lay with the relatively newly formed Open University (OU).

The OU operated a distance learning programme that suited me perfectly. I had become used to being responsible for my own learning schedule during the early days of my studies, but I also needed the support of the highly structured learning material that the OU provided. The OU system of study I followed consisted of taking a number of modules. By taking modules that were directly related to my previous studies for teacher training, the OU awarded me points for previous learning. I could obtain a basic non-honours bachelor degree within three years, if I could maintain the demanding schedule I had set myself.

I liked the structured approach of the OU, with set text books and well prepared course material, backed by superb taped radio programmes. There were also early morning and late night television programmes you could watch, if you could cope with the unsociable hours that they were transmitted. The beauty of the system from my point of view was that I could do the reading and preparation work just when it suited me. I could also record the television programmes and watch them at a time convenient to me.

I enjoyed the rigour of producing essays and computer marked assignments. A definite plus for me was that assessment work was always returned before the next assignment had to be written, so you always knew where you stood with regard to assessment. It was even possible to work out your overall performance on the course by averaging out assessment scores. The whole system was truly "open", not just from the point of view of access but also in relation to assessment.

One of the modules I took with the OU was a study of psychology, and some of the other modules I studied also contained chunks of psychology. I found this the most interesting aspect of my degree course, so much so, that I began to direct most of my non-academic reading in this direction. I was given copies of Freud's

241

Introductory Lectures on Psycho-Analysis, The Interpretation of Dreams, and *The Psychopathology of Everyday Life* as presents. I found them addictive and they surely should only be embarked upon by someone who has the time to read them without having to give diverted attention to dashing off essays.

An integral part of my OU course was that students were required to spend one week at a "Summer School". These took place on a university campus while the normal students were on their summer break. This not only gave OU students the opportunity to experience campus life, but also exposed them to full-time intensive study.

I chose to attend a summer school at Bath University, simply because it was in a geographical area I wanted to visit. Little was I to know that Bath University was to play an important part in my later academic life.

Summer school at Bath was truly a taster of university life, but for many of the middle-aged OU students it was like a second youth for them. Some of the so called "mature" students really looked on it as an escape from their home life and an opportunity to flirt and carry on while out of the sight of their spouses. Perhaps this was how they imagined normal full-time students behaved, but at times the behaviour was immature and embarrassing to observe. However, all-in-all, it was a good and varied week, but it did not really reflect the true university life I was to experience later in my life.

The OU examinations were very thorough and demanding; all aspects were clearly related to the course work we had covered; there were no hidden elements that you could question and ask, "What relationship has this to my studies?" I really enjoyed the buzz of the examinations because the studies I had done prepared me thoroughly for them. And the results came through relatively quickly. I was thrilled to learn that I had passed each year of study, especially the final year of the course, and to know I would now have the coveted letters "BA" after my name.

My degree ceremony took place at Alexandra Palace in Wood Green, London. A more beautiful place could not have been chosen. It was a huge building with a long terrace commanding views right across London to the North Downs. My wife and my two daughters came with me to the ceremony. As the event was televised my parents could also watch at home, because the tickets for guests to attend the ceremony were limited.

I was delighted to wear a gown at last, although I was a little disappointed that a mortar board did not feature in the regalia. I was surprised that some of the graduates chose not to wear a gown, although there was a hire charge and some may have found this a cost they could not afford. But I was particularly surprised that some people took no effort to dress for the occasion, with some appearing to deliberately "dress down". It seemed a little sad to me to attend a ceremony that is after-all about pomp and tradition, and turn up in jeans and a scruffy T-shirt.

While attending some in-service courses as part of my work as a teacher, I frequently met so-called academics who criticised the OU, accusing it of "spoon feeding" its students, although they were not averse to using OU material in their own lectures. During my later studies for higher degrees I could understand why the OU could have been said to "spoon feed" its students, but I still maintain the criticism was totally unjust. No time was wasted pursuing material that was irrelevant to the course; consequently a greater volume of relevant knowledge was obtained. The assessment procedures were most regular and rigorous, and compared favourably with my later higher degree work. And they certainly could not have been said to spoon feed me when I later did my Ph.D. with the OU as one of their earlier doctorates.

I recognise that the OU degree course work did not require as much search for information as my later studies for a higher degree, but I still maintain that it provided a sound basis for my research work. And I am sure that had I continued my first degree to honours level it would have been even more demanding.

Only a year after completing my bachelor degree I realised that the bug for learning was even stronger than ever. I decided that I would like to study for a higher degree, but this seemed an impossible dream. To do this meant full-time study, and grants were not available for higher degree study, or were they? The glimmer of a possibility lay with my employers, Essex County Council. They were at that time offering a small selection of teachers a year's secondment to study for a higher degree. In effect it meant that if I were successful in my application, I would receive a year off work on full pay to study, and my tuition fees would be met by the local education authority. This was too good an opportunity to miss, if I could get selected from the many applicants.

I applied for the one year secondment and, after a nail-biting wait, I was told that if I found a university to accept me, I could go. But there was one problem. All the universities I obtained information from had an entry requirement of a "good honours degree". I didn't have an honours degree let alone a "good one", whatever that was! My bachelor degree had only been taken to basic level — I had not elected for further studies in order to convert it to an honours degree. But I had been successful in the past when I had not had the right entry requirements and had made an application anyway, so why couldn't I be successful again? The two master's degree courses that particularly appealed to me were offered by the universities of Bath and Cambridge. Yes, Cambridge! Why not?

I sent applications off to both of these prestigious institutions giving them details of my studies to date. I was fully expecting both of them to write back pointing out their entry procedures required a good honours first degree. Cambridge wrote asking me to write a paper and send it to them for assessment, and Bath invited me for an interview.

I produced the paper and sent it off to Cambridge and, while waiting for a response to this, the date for my interview at Bath arrived. As I started out on the long journey from Essex to Bath my buoyant attitude began to deflate. I was full of doubts. What was the point in going all that way (a round trip of more than 300 miles) only to be told to come back when you have an honours degree? But I felt that I had to give it a try. Olivia had been caught up in my enthusiasm, and my bosses at work had given me the day off work to attend the interview, so I went on with what seemed a venture doomed to failure.

When I arrived at the office of the professor who was to interview me, his secretary apologised and said he was delayed and would be with me as soon as possible. This seemed an ominous start to me. I waited for a full hour before he arrived. When he came into the office he was apologising profusely for his late arrival, and in the same breath he was telling me he couldn't give me much time because he had a lecture to deliver in twenty minutes. This seemed reminiscent of the time when I applied for entry to teacher training. My immediate thoughts were, "I've been down this road before. I'm in with a chance here."

I was surprised when very soon into the interview the professor began asking me which of the variety of options within the course I would like to take. This seemed to imply that I was being offered a place, but I thought I needed to ask the direct question to be sure this was the case. The confirmation made my spirits soar. I could start next term. It was unbelievable.

I was later to receive an offer of a place at the more prestigious Cambridge University for the year following the placement at Bath. But I decided to stick with Bath.

This turned out to be a wise decision because the opportunities for a secondment became very rare following my year at Bath. But anyway, as it turned out, I could not possibly have been as happy as I was at Bath University.

It was September 1978. I was now nearly thirty-eight years of age, married with two children, and embarking on yet another academic experience, at the highest level for me so far. This time it was to be different in many ways. I would be living away from my family and attending a "real" university. And I would be relatively well off financially, thanks to the generosity of my employers. I was going on full pay, and my tuition fees and accommodation would be paid for. I only had to meet my end of term travel costs and daily living expenses. These would be financed by income from academic books I had begun to have published.

I had chosen to live on campus. I did this partly to enjoy the feel of being in a conventional university, but also because I didn't want to waste any time travelling to and from the university. I was determined to make the most of this opportunity and there was going to be no time-wasting for me during this year.

I was allocated a top room in a block of eight rooms with seven other young men. I was by far the oldest in our "house". I was to be a "wrinkly" yet again. There was a communal kitchen that was sparsely but adequately equipped, with a dining area large enough for us all to eat together if we wished. We also shared a bathroom with toilets and showers. A lady came in

247

daily to clean through the building and our rooms, although not at the weekends.

At first sight my room seemed a bit like a prison cell, with plain block-work walls. But as far as I was concerned it was very practicable. A good-sized window let in a generous amount of light, and the view was into wooded parkland. The bed was comfortable and there was a desk with a reading light that was ideal for the late night studying I anticipated. The wardrobe and set of drawers that was provided was adequate for the limited clothes I had brought with me. And there was a good bookshelf for my reference books. All in all, I felt that I was adequately provided for in material needs to face the hard slog ahead, but I just hoped that my academic ability was also adequate.

The other young students in my house were all studying various bachelor degree courses. I was the only post graduate in the house. One black lad in the house was from a high status, wealthy African family, and he was already assured of an important government position on return to his homeland. He had a delightful personality and was always laughing about something. We got on well together and he had a stream of young ladies calling on him. With his offbeat sense of humour, it wasn't surprising that he was so popular. One day he said to me very seriously, "If you don't know where you're going, Alan, you might end up somewhere else!"

One other lad in the house was from Turkey. I was told by the other residents that he rarely attended lectures or presented assignments. He kept failing

248

exams and was clearly not going to get a degree. But he maintained his place in the university, I was told, because his family were wealthy enough to continue paying his fees. So, he seemed to have become a long-term student. I don't know if this was true, but if it was it seemed an awful waste of a university place.

Over a period of several weeks we found that the cutlery and crockery were disappearing from the kitchen. Eventually there was not enough for more than two people to have a meal at one time. The remainder of the occupants of the house maintained that the Turkish lad had taken them. I found it hard to believe that someone from such a wealthy background would commit such petty stealing in this way. However, the house master responsible for the student accommodation was called in.

The house master arrived with a set of master keys while the Turkish lad was elsewhere. He opened the boy's door with the other residents present as witnesses. Inside was the foulest mess I have ever seen. The chap had been making meals in the kitchen and taking them back to his room to eat. And there was the crockery and cutlery for the whole house strewn around his room, with parts of meals on them green with mould. He was obviously not used to cleaning up after himself! The rest of the residents insisted that they would not live in the same house as this young man and he was moved off campus, and presumably lived happily ever after in squalor.

It was no wonder I loved being at Bath. It is one of Britain's oldest cities, famous since Roman times for its warm mineral springs. The Roman baths are among the best preserved in England. It was a beautiful area with many celebrated features of architecture that drew students from all over Europe. The mixture of its Roman origins and Georgian architecture presented many opportunities to explore, if time from studying allowed it.

I was enraptured by the university as a great centre of learning. I loved the challenges it set me, and the opportunities it provided to enrich my life. I enjoyed mixing with students from far-flung places, and I appreciated the tutors I worked with who did so much to inspire me. I had the feeling that I was in a place that could provide the important destiny of many people, and this was so.

I worked hard from the very start of my first term, and I was delighted to find how much of the knowledge and skills I had picked up on my OU course helped me. Halfway through my first term everything was beginning to come together nicely. I found that I was not only equal to any of the other students on the course, but many of them came to me for advice and guidance.

There were students alongside me on my course at Bath from all the four corners of the world. I was now friends with mature students from Africa, Argentina, Australia and New Zealand, Iran, Iraq, Malaysia, China, Singapore and many European countries. Today it seems inconceivable that Britain has been involved in conflicts with several of these countries, and my ex-student colleagues would have considered me an "enemy" at some time since we studied together, but they all enriched my life in many ways and I shall always treasure the friendship we shared.

In later years, following the Falklands War, and while reminiscing on my friendships with students from Argentina, some wag said to me, "We may have bloodied the Argies noses, but they'll get their own back. You mark my words. They'll take all the keys off the tins of corned beef." But in effect they got their revenge through "the hand of God" in a football match!

Several of us began a weekly ritual of cooking a meal for guests from other countries. In this way we all became familiar with the home cooking of others. It was quite a challenge to prepare a traditional English meal without including a content (e.g. cow) that was unacceptable to some of the guests that had been invited.

Groups of students were invited to elect a fellow student to attend Senate committee meetings on their behalf. The representative would put to the committee any grumbles or suggestions they may have. It was normal to have a separate representative of the overseas students. I was touched and honoured when the overseas contingent insisted that they only wanted me as their elected representative, despite my protestations that they should choose one of their own to represent them. I was also invited to some wonderful parties where I was the only white person present.

An interesting aspect of my master's degree course was that, although there were lectures and seminars where your presence was expected, there were many others that you could attend that were not directly related to your chosen options. I attended some sessions related to parapsychology. These may not have contributed to my assessment work, but they provided me with a fascinating insight into this often maligned element of psychology, and far removed from the charlatans often associated with it sensationally.

An important development of these extra-curricular aspects of my course was that it allowed me access to groups practising psychotherapy, which enabled me to extend my skills in this area. It had now become my long-term aim to practice psychotherapy. As part of this personal development I also took courses in hypnotherapy, which I quickly found to be a useful tool in therapy.

I "cut my teeth" on fellow students but soon found that many others from outside the university fraternity were coming on campus to visit me for therapy. It became important that I did not allow this development to interfere with my studies. Quite interestingly those who came for therapy were predominantly women. It appeared that women were more willing to discuss their problems than men. The relatively few men that did come for therapy gave me the impression that they, unlike the women, considered their psychological problems as a sign of weakness.

The kind of problems experienced by the people who came for therapy were very varied. Several recognised that they had obsessions that were adversely affecting their life. One lady was largely confined to her home because she was constantly worried about going anywhere in case she was unable to find a toilet, even though she didn't necessarily need to use one. Another was suffering from obsessive compulsion disorder (OCD) which caused her to constantly wash her hands. This meant that the preparation of a simple meal would take many hours.

As previously mentioned, I was introduced to the use of hypnotherapy as a useful tool in psychotherapy. Until then my only experience of hypnotherapy was seeing it used in stage shows. Now I learnt how to use it constructively, and it has become a permanent part of my treatment programme today.

The standard procedure for assessment of our work on the course was clearly structured. We would attend a number of lectures and seminars associated with the modules we had chosen to study. Set reading would be provided prior to each lecture enabling us to participate in discussions if the reading had been carried out. After several lectures the assignment for the module was issued, and we would be given some direction to help structure our work, and a submission date was set. We would be tackling three such assignments at one time.

After the submission date, but before the assignment was assessed and returned to us, we would meet our tutors as a group and the basic content of the assignment we had submitted was discussed. One black African student, whose name no one could pronounce, complained, "Dis is like medicine after death." Thereafter he was always referred to as "Medicine after Death". We could pronounce that.

There were tutors who I found I particularly enjoyed working with. One such person was an elderly professor who many of my fellow students found difficult to follow. But I seemed to tune straight into what he was getting at, and we did some excellent research together. I gained my first ever "A" grade and a distinction as a result of work I submitted to him. One day he said to me in his gentle, kindly manner, "Always remember, Alan, knowledge is knowing a tomato is a fruit, but wisdom is knowing not to include tomato in a fruit salad."

I also hit it off with my tutor for psychology. My expertise in this subject was now at a level where I could discuss most aspects of it with him on an even footing, and there were even areas that I could explain for his benefit. He chose me to lead many of the seminars with other students. Preparation for these seminars did much to extend my experience in forming my own approaches to psychological practice.

I was taking one such psychology seminar, for which prior reading had been set. Early in the seminar I posed some questions to the group to identify those who had understood the reading. My intention was to use those appearing knowledgeable to expand the discussions. One of the youngest girls in the group gave me an intelligent response and, assuming that she had read thoroughly, I chose to use her to expand the discussion. But, other than her initial response, she could not offer any further contribution. Later I questioned her privately about this. She told me frankly that she had not done the reading that had been set, and the early answer she had given me had been gleaned from the "agony aunt" column from a popular women's

254

magazine only that morning. I was surprised that someone would try to study at master's level in this off-hand way, and not surprisingly the girl dropped out of the course part way through.

Towards the end of the first term the chill of winter crept in. One of the overseas students I frequently worked closely with was a young girl called Sauk (pronounced "Sock") from Singapore. She was excited at the prospect of seeing snow for the first time in her life. One day there was an urgent hammering on my door. I opened the door to find Sauk there in a state of high excitement. "Come quickly, Alan, there is snow." I went out into the garden to see everything glittering white — with a heavy frost. But she was to get a wonderful experience of snow early in the next term, when we had falls that lay heavy for two weeks and isolated the university for several days.

An important element of the course was to submit a dissertation on a topic negotiated with one of the tutors we worked with during the first two terms. The work on the dissertation was to be the main task for the third and final term, and the work had to include considerable elements of pure research.

The two obvious choices for me were the area I had explored with the professor I had hit it off so well with, or the doctor who guided me through the work of my favourite subject, psychology. I chose the latter, particularly because the area I wanted to research was clearly pure psychology, and I now knew that this was the area in which I wanted to work in due course.

My supervisor was very constructive, but extremely demanding. During our early meetings he guided the structure of my work carefully so that, if I decided to continue my work to take a doctorate, my current work could form the basis of further research. At that time studying for a doctorate could not have been further from my thoughts, but one never knows for sure what the future holds!

My supervisor also talked about the tough time his supervisor had given him while he was doing his doctorate at Cambridge University. I thought to myself, "I reckon you are going to give me a tough time." I was right. But he was always constructive and the contribution he made to my academic development was invaluable.

The general area of my research was to investigate disruptive behaviour at the secondary level of education. As a pilot study I was investigating various aspects of the views of teachers and comparing them with what other researchers were stating was the case. I also gathered data on the incidence and form that such behaviour took; the differences between age groups, and many other relevant aspects. I would also identify the possible psychological factors behind disruptive behaviour.

When it came to analysis of the data I had collected from six secondary schools in Essex, my supervisor directed me to two other doctors who specialised in statistical analysis. This was very new to me. Some analysis needed to be carried out by computer, but this was still in its early stages of widespread use, although

Bath University was well advanced in making their use open to as many students as possible. My two additional advisors gave me considerable time and guidance, and they introduced me to tests of significance and probability. They also taught me how to analyse the confusing mass of data the computer printed out overnight.

I had now moved into a completely different phase in my academic development. I was enjoying the new knowledge and experience, but it was a strenuous time. From early morning until late at night my time was devoted entirely to work. I sacrificed all socialising, determined that my dissertation would be a success. I lost a lot of weight during this term. Nervous energy and skimpy meals were the culprits.

During the occasional meetings I had with other students on my course we compared the progress of our work. I soon realised that the path I was following was very different from any of their work, and I seemed to be the only one working with three tutors. But right to the last day my tutors harried, questioned and probed, until I thought I would burst with frustration. However, they drew the best out of me and I will be forever grateful to them.

Then one day my personal supervisor told me it was done. I could now get my work typed and bound. I employed one of the university secretaries to key the manuscript in her spare time. Each day she would give me a batch of work she had typed. I would proofread her typing and return errors for correction. Some of the formulae symbols could not be produced by a typewriter and these had to be entered by hand. Once we had everything faithfully recorded I handed the typescript into the photocopying department to make the requisite number of copies. Finally, the work went to the binding department where the final process would be carried out.

When I handed over my bound copies of the work I could scarcely believe it was all finished. I was completely exhausted but confident that my course work and my dissertation would assure my success at master's level. All I now wanted was to say farewell to my many new friends from around the world and get home to my family, assured that I had reached the zenith of my academic career. Or had I?

The ceremony for the presentation of my master's degree took place one year later in the famous eighteenth century pump-rooms adjoining the Roman baths, with the magnificent abbey standing nearby. It was a truly beautiful place to have the degree presented. My wife and my two daughters attended. By this time my wife had obtained her bachelor degree with London University, so we were able to have a photo taken with both of us in caps and gowns together with our daughters. Later our daughters both also obtained bachelor and master's degrees, and by then friends had begun to refer to us as the "four degrees".

By the end of my master's degree course I was convinced that I never wanted to do any more academic work. The course had exhausted me. But my dissertation work had left me with a feeling of some unfinished business to do. It was only a very short time after my master's degree ceremony that I began to investigate the possibility of extending the pilot study I had carried out at Bath. I could now see how the structure that my supervisor had wisely guided me to follow would lend itself to a doctoral thesis, and I decided that I needed to take this last step or I would always be wondering if I could have done it.

I would no longer have the luxury of a secondment. I would have to be self-financing. I would also have to carry out my research while continuing my work as a teacher. For these reasons, it seemed that a conventional university might not be the best option for me, but the OU would, again, fit the bill nicely. I decided to send a proposal to the OU. This took the form of an extension of my pilot research work carried out at Bath.

In due course I was interviewed by an extremely young professor, five years younger than myself. He was internationally famous for statistical analysis and he was happy to supervise this aspect of my proposed research programme, but he was out of his depth with regard to the psychological element. We reached a compromise. If I could find a university supervisor for the psychological elements, and if I could tolerate having two supervisors, the OU would take me on as one of their earliest doctorate students.

I wrote to one of the London University colleges outlining the proposed structure for my thesis, and explaining my need for a supervisor familiar with education and psychology. In due course I was put in touch with a lady doctor willing to act as co-supervisor with the OU professor. The prospect of going forward was looking more positive.

It took several months of negotiation to create a structure for my research work that satisfied both of my supervisors. This was finally agreed at a meeting at the OU headquarters at Milton Keynes. At the meeting the professor told me that when he did his doctorate at Cambridge, his supervisor (the same as that of my supervisor at Bath) had given him a very tough time. I thought to myself, "I've been down this path before. You're going to give me a tough time also." I was right again.

The basis of my thesis was similar to the pilot study I had created at Bath, but the work would be extended in several ways. My sample would be bigger; more schools, more teachers. My research questionnaire would be refined to eliminate snags that had occurred in the earlier work. The statistical analysis would have to be far more rigorous to satisfy the specialist knowledge of the professor. In addition, I was to carry out research into behaviour modification techniques aimed at dealing with disruptive behaviour. This was to be focused on the fourteen- to sixteen-year-old pupils, which my master's degree research had identified as causing secondary teachers most concern. I was also intending to carry out some in-depth case studies linking my research findings with the reality of the classroom situation. My work would also make recommendations to help those faced with dealing with such behaviour problems in schools.

260

I was now working during the day at my teaching job, continuing with school work in the early evening, off to practice judo three or four evenings a week, coming home from judo about 10.15p.m., studying until 1.00a.m., then off to bed. Up again the next morning at 6.30a.m. to repeat the whole thing again. Weekends were spent catching up on school work, studying, writing, and trying to make some contribution to the maintenance of our large house and huge garden. My wife was also now teaching full-time.

The regime I had adopted was punishing, but I was able to keep up with the workload because I had good health and abundant energy. I recognised this as the key to success. I was enthused with my research and the limitless learning I had been given access to. I worked longer and longer hours to fit everything in and enjoyed every minute of it, blessed with the devoted support of Olivia and my two daughters. But it was all becoming too much to keep up with. It was clear that I was doing too much, and if I didn't create more time my doctorate work would flounder. I realised that the time had come to retire from judo, a sport I had been practising for twenty years.

My doctorate research was, as one might expect, more demanding than any academic work I had undertaken before. The pattern of the work I had established with my supervisors was that as I completed blocks of research, I would write these up and submit my work to both supervisors. When I had received their responses I would re-write the work, incorporating or acting upon their suggestions, and submit it again for further observations. Not surprisingly conflicts of views occurred as any top-flight academic researcher will readily confirm.

My lady supervisor and I hit it off immediately and we were clearly both on the same wavelength. Her constructive criticism kept me firmly focused and she was relentlessly demanding, as you would expect working at the leading edge of new knowledge. But no matter how harsh her criticism, she was always constructive and encouraging, and somehow within her criticism she always managed to raise my enthusiasm.

My young professor was equally demanding but less encouraging than my other supervisor. We saw eye to eye with regard to the statistical analysis aspects of my research, but we clashed when my work could not be verified on a statistical basis. It was then, and still is, my view that human behaviour cannot always be unequivocally assessed by statistics. And it was in this respect we continually crossed swords.

Within my thesis I included specific case studies of individuals that, in my view, allowed qualified conclusions to be drawn. These conclusions did not claim to be completely objective, but they could be compared within the sample I had investigated, and they could be compared with the findings of other researchers. Unfortunately this did not satisfy my professor — he wanted statistical analysis that supported, or otherwise, the conclusions I had reached.

The essence of these case studies culminated in a particular chapter of my thesis. At a crucial, crunch meeting with the professor, close to the conclusion of my work, he asked me to delete this particular chapter from my work. If I did this he said he would not stand in the way of the final submission of my thesis. I was so convinced of the important relevance of the case studies to my work that I refused to delete them. The alternative was to submit my thesis with it noted with the professor's concerns. I chose this course of action, fully realising that I was taking a big gamble.

In due course I was given the date of my viva — the oral grilling inquisition by my examiners. I travelled to the OU headquarters at Milton Keynes, accompanied by my ever supportive lady supervisor. The young professor had declined to attend and had made his reasons known to my examiners.

In due course I sat in the examination room and faced the three visiting professors from far-flung universities who were to examine me, and to decide the fate of almost four years of exhaustive work. They had clearly studied my work very thoroughly and the questions and answers flowed between us fast and furious. I lost all track of time but throughout the ordeal I knew that I was showing astute knowledge of my work. After what seemed like a lifetime it was done. I was given the opportunity to go home and wait for their decision, or I could wait in another room until they had finished their deliberations, with the warning that this could take several hours. I couldn't face the agonising wait at home and chose to stay until they had reached a decision.

In effect I had not even had time to begin to drink the coffee provided in the waiting room before I was summoned back into the examining room to learn my fate. There was no attempt to prolong my agony. Immediately I entered the room, the professor who had chaired the proceedings shook my hand and said, "I am delighted to tell you that you have now joined the elite circle of academics in the top percentile of academic achievement in the world." My relief and joy knew no bounds at that moment.

My joy was further heightened by the professor's next words. He said, "I understand that there was some disagreement with one of your supervisors with regard to Chapter Four of your thesis (the case studies). I have to tell you that chapter particularly impressed us all and it made a valuable contribution to your work." I felt vindicated. In a way I had gambled on what I believed in, and won.

On the drive home my joy was bubbling inside of me, but I was concerned that Olivia would be sick with worry not knowing the outcome. I asked my supervisor if she would mind if we interrupted our journey home to phone Olivia and give her the news, to which she readily agreed. In the public call box all I could blurt out was, "I got it, I got it."

One of the first people to telephone and congratulate me was my professor supervisor. He generously acknowledged that he had been mistaken about a key aspect of my work. Sadly my father was no longer alive to share the joy of my ultimate achievement, and not long after my final success, the young professor also died.

264

Part way through my doctorate research my father asked me to explain the purpose of doing a doctorate. He had assumed I was studying to become a general practitioner. He seemed almost disappointed when I explained that I aimed to practice as a psychologist. He died just six months before I completed my research.

My father's death came close to the end of my work, and it came at a time when I was experiencing particularly harsh conflict with the professor over the case studies issue. His death affected me badly and I had little interest in continuing the work. But my determination to finish and present my research came from Olivia, who convinced me that I should complete the work, especially for my father, but also because I owed it to my family who had also made considerable sacrifices during my work. It was this reasoning that motivated me to finish the job of going from "dole to doctorate" in sixteen years. Not bad for an Eleven-Plus failure!

CHAPTER
ELEVEN

CHANCE HAPPENINGS

I was always an avid reader from an early age. I read anything I could lay my hands on. Like most young boys, I started with school readers and comics, but they were soon found not to have enough content to satisfy my thirst for the printed word. Even the newspapers that came into our house, when I was young, failed to hold my interest for long. I was always searching for reading material that would stretch my mind.

From an early age, books were my most valuable Christmas presents. Some books were read time and again. Sir Arthur Conan Doyle's *The Lost World* and Johann Wyss' *The Swiss Family Robinson* were firm favourites, read many times. A more adult book that appealed to me was Samuel Butler's *Erehwon*, although it was not until in my late teens that I realised that the title spelt "Nowhere" backwards. These are the kind of books I wolfed down in my formative years.

I had never considered becoming a writer, and it was purely by chance that I ended up writing more than thirty books. These books eventually caused me to visit many places in the world that I may never have visited, and made me many new friends and acquaintances, but it took a series of chance happenings for this to come about.

When I first began my teaching career, the school leaving age had recently been raised from fifteen years of age to sixteen. Prior to this the main public examination for this age group was the General Certificate of Education (GCE) "O" level, which was only taken by a relatively small proportion of the schools' population. Now there were many more youngsters in the education system for longer, and the Certificate of Secondary Education (CSE) was introduced to provide a lower level of examination for the large number of school pupils who were not able to cope with the more demanding GCE. England now had a dual level of examinations. Surely this was a recipe for discord?

The school where I was employed had recently changed its status from a grammar school to a comprehensive. Classes now contained a wider range of ability. In one class there were the more able pupils who were destined to take the GCE, and also others who would take the easier CSE. But in the same class were those children who would struggle even with the lower level exam. This was a challenge for all those involved with teaching fourteen- to sixteen-year-olds, many of whom were disgruntled with having to do an extra year of schooling anyway.

One of the subjects I taught this age group was commerce, an earlier form of business studies. Initially this had only been a GCE subject, but was now available for CSE also. This was the case with a wide range of subjects, and the CSE made the task of teaching mixed ability classes a little more manageable, but an important difficulty remained.

Although the dual examination system helped teachers considerably, many of the existing text books were written for the higher standard of the GCE. Some books were written especially for the CSE level of pupils, but this left teachers with two problems. First they needed to buy two sets of books to meet the full range of ability, and they did not have the funds to do this. Second, it was not always possible to say what level a pupil was capable of. Some bordered between the two, and some would possibly not take any examination. There was clearly a need for texts that were sufficiently demanding for the GCE student, but also straightforward enough to meet the needs of the less able pupil and the CSE. This would enable the decision of choice of examination to be made as late as possible, which was more beneficial to everyone.

Like most heads of departments, I could only afford to finance a single set of books. There was a commonly used text for commerce at that time, written by a well-established author of business related books. The content of his book was very comprehensive, but pupils below the "O" level standard struggled with it. In addition, being almost devoid of illustrations, it failed to interest the lower ability pupil who needed graphics to draw their attention.

I began to re-write chapters of this book in a language that the full range of ability could understand, but maintaining the fullness of content the writer had

268

included. I also included illustrations to draw the interest of the lower ability reader, and made these suitable for posing questions to extend knowledge and understanding. In addition, I devised a collection of exercises to go with each chapter consisting of a mixture of CSE and GCE type of activities.

I recreated a few chapters of this book in this way. I got volunteer typists to type them onto ink duplicating masters and created a number of booklets to trial with my pupils. They worked well and, together with my volunteer typists, we created eight booklets from as many chapters of the traditional book. These made a world of difference to my pupils and I found that I could now teach the full range of ability using my single resource material. When it came to exam time our results showed that the material was proving a success, and certainly the pupils were happier with it.

Purely by chance, I sent a letter to the author of this traditional book, care of his publishers, sending him some sample chapters of the work I had created. In my letter I suggested to him that he might consider re-writing his book in this style, and I offered to send him the other chapters I had re-written.

He generously wrote back to me, returning my material, and advising me to write my own book, and telling me that the material I had created would market well. I replied explaining to him that I didn't want to write a book, and questioned why he would want to encourage me to compete against him. He replied again, asserting that if his work was not strong enough to hold its share of the market, he did not deserve it.

He again urged me to approach a publisher with my work. I was grateful for this man's honest encouragement and decided that perhaps I would try to get my work published.

I wrote to Pitman Publishing, who were worldwide leaders in business publications, and sent samples of my work. I received a polite, "Thanks, but no thanks" response from them and shelved the idea, without even considering approaching other publishers. I continued to write booklets for my pupils and I had by now established my own distinct, direct style of writing and constructive graphics.

During this period of my teaching career, whilst still continuing to teach in the school where I was employed, the education authorities had begun to use me to deliver in-service training courses for other teachers in centres around the county of Essex. While running a course in one such centre, a publishing agent happened to be visiting, and he sat in on one of my lectures. He asked me if I had ever considered writing. I explained about the material I had created and of my rejection by Pitman. He asked if I would allow him to become my agent, for which he would take 2 per cent of my 12 per cent royalties. I accepted the offer and, in due course, I sent him a copy of the work I had produced, and then forgot all about it.

One day I received a telephone call from him. He said, "I have good news and bad news. The bad news is that I can no longer act as your agent. The good news is that I have been appointed publishing director of a large publishing company, which precludes me from acting as your agent, but the first project I want to undertake is to publish your book." The even better news was that I would now receive the whole 12 per cent of the royalties. Another chance happening!

Now I became keen to see my name in print and to see the work I had created for my students published. Thoughts of earning income from my work were far from my mind, and I would probably have agreed to have it published for no income at all. Then I received a cheque for £500 as a royalty advance, and the possibility of a small income became attractive.

And so my first book was published with Thomas Nelson. The process of working with editors and artists was very stimulating, and I was fortunate in that the people with whom I worked seemed to interpret perfectly the style and format that I was trying to achieve. My female editor (nearly all my editors have been ladies) gently nudged me into ways to improve my work, and helped me realise ways to make my work less male-orientated. Sexual equality was becoming the "in thing" and there were lessons I needed to learn.

My first book was published after months of waiting, during which I became anxious about the reception it would get. It was going to be very different from anything currently on the market at that time. But I need not have worried. It was an immediate and outstanding success and the first print sold out rapidly, much to the delight of my publishers. It was clear that the style of presentation of the content of my book was a key factor in its exciting success.

Academic books can be boring for young people, especially if they are not particularly inspired by the subject they are studying. Unfortunately, it is too often the case that many young people going through puberty are not enthusiastic about much of their learning. This represents a major challenge for academic writers.

I made my books more interesting, not only by a direct style of writing, but also by surprising the reader by interjecting little sources of amusement, without detracting from the value of the learning material. For example, the subject Accounts is necessarily very dominated by numbers and names. To liven up the text I included amusing names. So the reader would be studying a serious or difficult topic and suddenly come across names such as D. Caffenate, I. Moan, T. Bags, D. Tail, Polly Styrene, B. Generous, Miss Chief, Miss Take, Dandy Lion, and so on. Consequently, I frequently get letters from teachers and students expressing their glee at this minor kind of amusement interjected into their learning.

It became a family pastime thinking up amusing names while driving along the motorway. Sometimes the names were real and were spotted on passing vehicles, and sometimes they were a figment of our imagination. The list became endless and the fun limitless. Soon we were extending the names to business names. All of this was the source of good fun for the reader, and lightened up their learning. For example, can you imagine the merchandise or services provided by the following businesses: Fruits N Roots, Ladies in Waiting, Sticky Fingers, Bustit & Wreckit, Mr

Dingo, and fast food outlets such as The Sizzling Sausage, The Runaway Chicken, The Burnt Burger.

I was soon contracted to write three more business related books. I expected that, having established a good rapport with my first editor, I would be working with her on my second book. But she left and I was now working with another lady, with whom I also got on well, and she also further guided the development of my writing skills.

As I have said, nearly all of the many editors I have worked with have been females. In some way or other they have each contributed to the development of my publishing experience. They opened my eyes to the need to include a multi-racial element into my work, and to recognise that women should feature equally with men. Unfortunately, being more academic and not so teenager-orientated, they did not all recognise the value of including humorous names such as those previously mentioned, and sometimes it took heated exchanges to get them included in a book.

The one occasion I worked with a male editor, resulted in one of my most horrendous experiences. It was an author's worst nightmare! I had contracted to write two books, on two examination subjects, at the same time. I had brought the books to a satisfactory conclusion at the same time and passed them to this young man. The normal procedure which I had become familiar with involved following a set pattern. I would, in due course, receive the editor's suggested corrections back. We would then discuss any changes suggested until we reached a conclusion to our mutual

273

satisfaction prior to the next stage in production. But, on this occasion, this did not happen. At that time I was very busy finalising the work on my doctorate so I was quite happy not to be harassed by my editor.

One day without prior warning I received the page proofs of my two books, and the correction stages seemed to have been completely omitted. When I began to read the page proofs the most horrific picture began to emerge. In comparing the page proofs with the manuscript I had submitted, it was clear that whole lumps of text had been deleted, but nothing had been inserted to replace it. This occurred throughout the two books. Whenever I tried to contact my editor to discuss the situation he always seemed to be "out of the office", and my calls were not returned.

In a state of exasperation I spoke to my editor's superior. My original manuscript was examined and it was realised that my young editor had blanked out areas of text throughout both books, but had not replaced the deleted wording, so many sections no longer made sense. Fortunately, I had copies of the original manuscript, and I was allocated another editor (a very young lady who was excellent to work with) and the projects were worked through again. I never learnt why the original editor vandalised my work in this way. It was never clear whether he truly made an error, or if it was an act of deliberate sabotage, I never found out. Apparently my books were not the only ones he treated in this way. He was fired, and I was safely returned to the realm of the lady editors.

274

The next book I was asked to write was for the Caribbean market. It was suggested that there would be a good demand for my work in that region, and several further books could result from the development. An editor responsible for the Caribbean region was sent to try and spark my interest in working on these projects. At that time I was rounding off my doctorate work ready for presentation, and with four books already in publication this seemed sufficient to satisfy my needs. It was my turn to say, "Thanks, but no thanks." But I was destined to work in the Caribbean region in the future, and it was to become an important part of my life.

Shortly after I had wrapped up my doctorate work I was contacted by a publishing director of Pitman Publishing, the company who had rejected my first book. He wanted me to consider writing for Pitman. I explained that I was content with my current publishers, and was ready for a rest from academic stress. He persuaded me to go in to London to have lunch with him, just to "talk about what the education market needed in the form of business books". Never being one to miss up an opportunity to tell anyone who would listen what help teachers needed, I decided to go and meet this man. So, I travelled into London for our meeting.

I first asked why he had chosen to approach me, and how he had obtained my phone number. He told me that he had "happened" to meet a publisher from another well known (but unnamed) publishing company in Frankfurt Airport, and I was mooted as being the "in-person" in the field at that time. Perhaps this was intended to boost my ego and soften me up and, in retrospect it seems to have had that effect.

We spent a pleasant few hours discussing the kind of books needed for a changing education publishing market, including one for a new examination being created called the General Certificate of Secondary Education (GCSE), and the new subject Business Studies. This was going to demand a different approach for teachers and authors.

We then went out and had a most enjoyable lunch where the wine flowed freely (perhaps too freely for my own good). When we arrived back at his office there were four contracts laid out on his desk that had been prepared by his secretary while we were at lunch. I was invited to sign all or some of the contracts. With my brain addled by wine and my stomach full of good food, I signed all four. Fortunately as I had now completed my doctorate work I had the capacity to take on more writing, although perhaps not as much as I had been contracted for.

For the next eighteen months I worked as hard as I had ever done to fulfil the contracts and delivery schedules I had committed to. I had many different editors. They were all females and each of them was excellent to work with. All seemed very young, but without exception I enjoyed working with them. And not one of them blanked out text without consulting me first!

I subsequently wrote nine books for Pitman. As part of my work for them I was to visit Australia and Hong Kong to promote my books and gather ideas for other publishing possibilities. Another of my publishers was also keen to extend their market to Australia. I was asked to investigate the current Australian Business Studies books to see if any could be profitably adapted for the UK market. Three further books came out of this visit.

The trip to Hong Kong had an unexpected outcome. I discovered two books being marketed there that were blatant copies of the work of my own books. Even illustrations had been copied with no attempt to change them. Through Pitman, I challenged the authors for infringement of copyright, which they duly acknowledged. The books were eventually taken out of print and I received a compensation settlement. These were two of three cases of plagiarism I have experienced. One editor said to me, "One way of looking at it, Alan, is that it is a compliment that they think your work is so good that they want to pinch it." It was a compliment that I could do without. However, the icing on the cake was that quite a reasonable proportion of my personal expenses would be tax deductible for my trip to Australia and Hong Kong.

It was about this time I received my first contact with Moshe. He was a young man in his late teens from Malawi in Central Africa. He was using one of my books as part of his studies. Moshe wrote to me via one of my publishers. He explained the current stage of his academic achievements. He also described his family's economic background, which was very poor by any English standard. They walked four miles to collect water and had no electricity. Moshe was trying to enlist my help and guidance so that he could come to England and train as a teacher, in order to "go back to his country and help others to learn".

It was sad to have to write back and explain that his qualifications were far from sufficient to gain entry to a teacher training course in England. And it was clear from his financial background information that he could not provide the necessary funding even if he did have the appropriate qualifications.

I have readily undertaken charity work, not to prove what a good person I am, but because I have always tried to put something back into life in return for the good fortune I sometimes reap. I had been contributing money regularly to various charities for many years, but I had for some time wondered whether my contributions were reaching the intended recipients, or if they were being really effective. I also questioned how much of the money I donated was swallowed up by administrative costs. I now had the opportunity to ensure my charitable contributions were directly being put to good use.

I began sending regular sums of money to Moshe and his family to help them become more self-sufficient. In return I received frequent reports of exactly how my money had been used and the effect it was having. Photos were always sent as proof of this.

It was satisfying to know exactly where my help was actually ending up. It was also pleasing to realise how a relatively small sum in our terms could do so much for a family in a third world country. I got some satisfaction from knowing that some of the benefits of my writing were helping others as well as my own family. The friendship with Moshe and his family continues to this day.

I was once engaged by one of my publishers to write a monthly article for an academic journal, whose circulation was about as large as the blood supply of the average gnat. And so was the income I received from the work. The editor of the journal, for some obscure reason, found it hard to understand why I was reluctant to devote so much time each month to create one-off articles when I preferred to give that time to the development of my next book, which paid off much better. He also failed to comprehend why I considered it harder and more time consuming to write within a small space allocation.

My first twelve books were created on the earliest form of computer. It was called a typewriter. I would write out my work in long-hand, pass it to a lady (called a typist) who keyed a hard copy of the material. I would read her completed work, indicate any errors or changes required, and she would re-key the whole work, incorporating the changes required. We sometimes went through this process several times before the final work could be submitted to the publisher. We thought we were at the leading edge of technology!

My move to my third publisher was an unintended happening. In fact, I was not even aware that I had moved. Longman Publishing took over the ownership of some of Pitman's books. One of these was mine. So I was now employed by yet another publisher without having solicited to be so. But subsequent books for

Longman were to take me in a different direction, as you will see later.

Employment by a fourth publisher was not solicited by me either. I received a phone call from a publishing director of Stanley Thornes to ask if I would be interested in producing some books for them. These involved two specialist dictionaries, which was to be something completely new and stimulating for me. On a trip to Australia I also discovered two books already in print for other authors that would convert well to the British market with adaptation. So I contracted to do this work for Stanley Thornes also, sharing the royalties with the original authors. These again involved new publishing experiences for me.

At this time I was now employed by four publishers; fortunately they were not all demanding books at the same time. I was still employed full-time as a senior teacher. I now had fifteen texts in publication. The income from my writing was good compared to most part-time income, but I still needed my employment full-time as a senior teacher to make ends meet, as HM Inspector of Taxes had me firmly by the privates as he grasped my undergarments for every penny he could acquire from me.

I had been writing a new book on a kind of a half promise of a contract from one of my publishers. As the work became well advanced, the publishing editor who had suggested the work in the first place left the company. There was some delay in appointing a replacement, and the person in temporary charge was reluctant to issue a contract until the new person was in

280

office. So I was obliged to look for another publisher rather than waste the work I had done. The answer came in the form of Hodder & Stoughton who were to become my fifth publisher.

I was no longer counting the number of books I had in publication, but I had begun to only consider writing work that really appealed to my interest. Longman approached me to write a book specifically for the Caribbean market. Many of my existing books were marketed in other countries, but I had not written anything for a specific foreign market and I was now intrigued by the prospect of writing for the Caribbean. It seemed a bit of a coincidence that I was now going to be writing for an area that I had rejected many years before. As this development occurred just as I had retired from teaching, I had the time available to do the job properly and actually visit the area. But, due to the vagaries of our taxation system, it was necessary for me to expend considerable costs and time working on the project before the taxman would deign to make a contribution.

The taxman, probably justifiably, will not give a tax allowance against speculative work. In other words, tax allowances are only allowed against income from books already published. So, in the case of my Caribbean works, I was obliged to work for more than a year, and also carry out expensive trips to the Caribbean well ahead of receiving any help from HM Tax Inspector. But this was the way in which I fell in love with the paradise island of Barbados.

The Caribbean publishing market had suffered for some time from English academics writing books for their schools, to meet the requirements of examinations set by British universities. The situations were far from satisfactory. It too frequently didn't work. How could authors in England, however highly qualified and experienced in publishing, adequately hope to create texts suitable for a market with which they were not fully familiar? The region now wanted books preferably written by local authors familiar with local issues. In addition, the Caribbean region had begun to establish its own system of examinations.

Unfortunately, initially, there were only a limited number of local authors with the experience required to write the books needed. But an excellent compromise was reached. Overseas authors were encouraged to work with a local author on new books for the region. In this way, local authors became familiar with the intricacies of publishing, and overseas authors, such as me, were assisted in assuring that their books embraced local issues.

For this new project, I would be required to work with a local person acting as co-author. I had by now worked successfully in England with a co-author on several books, so I was quite familiar with this arrangement. The problem later materialised that I had not taken into account the logistics of exchange of material over a great distance.

The syllabus for the subject, the Principles of Business, was very similar to much of the work I had previously done for my existing books, but of course there were many local variations that I needed guidance on. Longman suggested a Caribbean academic in Jamaica who would act as co-author and check my work and give it a local "flavour" for a split of my royalties. I signed a contract for my standard delivery period of one year. This, in retrospect, was a mistake.

Although I had for some time been using a computer to create my work and to present disks to publishers, e-mail was relatively new. Neither I nor my Caribbean co-author had access to it. Consequently each chapter had to be written by me, sent by "snail mail" to the Caribbean author for editing and local additions, and then returned to me for further work. This clearly slowed the whole process up, and my co-author was not working at the blistering pace I set myself when working on a book. At the same time, I soon realised that the style of writing of my co-author was very different to my own. So when the work came back from my Caribbean co-author it had to be re-written to ensure the completed work was in a single style throughout. At this time it was not viable for me to travel to Jamaica to work face-to-face with this co-author.

Because of this situation, for the first time in my publishing career, my manuscript was presented six months behind the one year schedule I had set. But when the book came out it was an immediate and outstanding success. This success came about because the book not only comprehensively covered the syllabus, but presented a dry subject in an interesting manner, and was backed by a wide range of activities that drew on the interest of the student.

Shortly after the launch of this, my first book for the Caribbean market, the opportunity arose whereby I could, at the age of fifty-six, take early retirement from teaching. This enabled me to access a reduced teacher's pension early. The opportunity came at an excellent time. Now I could give more time to my writing, and to extending my psychology practice. It did not take much consideration to take up the offer.

Shortly after this development I was contracted by Heinemann, who were to become my sixth publisher. They wanted two books for the Caribbean market. I now liked the challenge of this new market, and I appreciated the enthusiastic response I was getting to my first book there.

For my second and third books for the Caribbean market, I was to work with a co-author, Gillian, from Barbados — a Bajan. I interviewed her in England and I felt sure we could work well together, even though she had not published before and her academic qualification didn't match those of my previous co-authors. Immediately we began working together I sensed she was on the same wavelength as me, and she had a sense of humour that would help to inject some lightness into our work. I knew we would get on well, but the question was, would she be able to keep up with the blistering pace I was accustomed to?

This time I was determined to work first-hand with my co-author as much as possible, despite the considerable expense involved. It was in this way that

284

Olivia and I discovered a place that has now become an important part of our lives. Together with my co-author, we developed a schedule whereby we would exchange as much work as possible by e-mail attachments, but that at crucial stages in the work Olivia and I would go to Barbados and stay with Gillian, or she would fly to England and stay with us in Canvey Island while we worked through difficult parts of the book.

Gillian turned out to be excellent to work with. E-mail became an essential part of my everyday life. Each evening I would send chapters off to Barbados as attachments, and the next morning my first early morning job would be to download chapters that had been returned to me. The most frustrating times were whenever my computer or that of my co-author was "down". The books were delivered to the publisher dead on time, which was how I liked my projects to conclude.

On our first trip to Barbados, Gillian was working as a teacher and, therefore, we could only work together on the book at night. In effect this worked out well from my point of view. We would work together in the evenings until we were too tired to continue. Early the next morning I would key the material we had sorted out the night before. When I had completed this, Olivia and I were free to do the normal tourist thing, and in the evening we would get back to the grind of work.

Both of these new books were also an immediate success in the Caribbean market. They also enabled us to discover the paradise island of Barbados in the most delightful way, as a local temporary resident rather than as a tourist. It is the most wonderful place to visit and work. In subsequent visits we really acclimatised to living there and truly became temporary residents.

Within this chapter it can be seen that many chance happenings have influenced the direction of my life. Indeed, throughout this book there have been other examples of events that have had this effect. However, often it has not just been a case of events taking control of my life. Often it has been a case of recognising opportunities and taking advantage of them.

CHAPTER
TWELVE

BE KIND TO BOOKS

When regular income began to come in from my books it was of course exciting, especially when comparing it to the many years of hardship we had gone through as a family. However, we were apprehensive that we might get too used to this sudden increase in our wealth. How would we cope if we became accustomed to the increased income and then it stopped, as we were sure it would?

Olivia and I discussed this and we resolved that income from my books should remain separate from our normal living expenses. The bulk of the extra income was regularly invested, although not necessarily very profitably because we were not willing to take too much risk — we'd suffered too much in the past to allow our hard earned success to slip through our fingers.

An important luxury we did allow ourselves was to purchase a small second home in Spain. Quite apart from the fact that the purchase price was relatively cheap compared to home ownership in England, it was to provide an important bolt-hole where we could retreat and unwind, away from the stressful lifestyle we were still living.

Whilst the income from my writing helped to transform our life by increasing our financial independence, it was not sufficient to enable us to retire from our teaching jobs. Consequently, our decision to not allow our new-found wealth to contribute to our living expenses meant that the pressure of our way of life was not reduced. For this reason the bolt-hole in Spain became increasingly important.

We are on very friendly terms with our "neighbours" in Spain, and we enjoy the mix of cultures when we have community meetings or parties. The community has a great caretaker-come-janitor who takes care of the facilities in the complex in Spain, such as the gardens and the pool. His name is Raffa. One day Raffa came to me and said, "Alan, you come with me. We drive into the mountains. You bring camera. Very good for looking." "Great," I said, "I'll get Olivia too." "No," Raffa replied, "only you come with camera. Many ladies to photo."

I went to see Olivia and explained that I was in a tricky position. I didn't want to offend Raffa, but there was no way that we could get naughty photos developed, but at the same time I didn't want to lose the photos we had already taken. Olivia came up with a brilliant idea. There was an old camera in the apartment, I would put a film in that and when I came back I could throw away the film with the incriminating evidence.

In due course I sat in Raffa's tiny Fiat Panda, a true sewing machine on wheels, and we headed for the hills.

Before long we left the *terra firma* of the road and followed a gravel track, climbing all the way with the Panda roaring in protest. In due course we left the track and Raffa took to a dried river bed. We were well away from civilisation as I knew it. Eventually we came to a stop with the sides of the dry river bank high on either side of the diminutive car. "Come, Alan. Bring camera," Raffa whispered. We clambered up the bank stealthily and as we came over the top, there in all their glory, was a group of elderly ladies picking strawberries!

I took the obligatory photos, and Raffa was given a massive tray of strawberries to take away. So what was all the mystery about? Why wasn't Olivia allowed to come? Well, apart from the fact that the Panda probably couldn't accommodate three people and the mountain of strawberries, Raffa wanted our bounty to be a surprise for all the ladies in the complex. This incident, funny though it is, perhaps illustrates how generous so many of the working class Spanish can be.

Although I had been to Australia many times during my time as a seaman, I really didn't take the opportunity to see and learn about the country, and rarely saw more than the port areas. But, as previously mentioned, my writing gave me the opportunity to visit Australia again and see more of that vast continent.

On the journey out to Australia we were to stop-over in Singapore, where I would visit the Ministry of Education and meet people involved in education at a variety of levels. This was to be my first visit to Singapore and, apart from the useful public relations promotion, it gave Olivia and me the chance to

289

experience this enormously successful little island while it still retained some of its original culture. It also gave us the opportunity to spend some time with our good friend, Sauk, from my university days in Bath.

We arrived at Changi Airport, which is surely one of the most attractive airports in the world. Just to wander around the airport is an experience worth flying into the country for. There cannot be many airports that boast massive indoor fishponds, surrounded by spectacular plant life that most garden centres would give a lot to be able to achieve. Visitors in transit can walk around in comfort and be entertained by the sheer splendour of the place designed like a giant park, with shops (and aircraft) galore.

Our Singaporean friend is a member of the prestigious Changi Beach Club and, courtesy of our friendship with Sauk we were able to stay there. It is situated at the eastern end of the island, near Changi Village, well out from the city. Changi Village is an area where the original culture of Singapore was still in evidence. The club was originally known just as The Changi Club and it existed for officers serving in the British Army. After the pullout of the British troops in the 1970s, the club was handed over to local control. The facilities it now offers are excellent and numerous. We were indeed fortunate to be able to spend some time there.

There are other pockets of the original culture in Singapore. For example, Chinatown is a relatively small area today that a long time back used to brim with half-starving immigrants from China. Today it is a highly popular place for visitors to go and haggle over handicrafts and antiques. Other ethnic centres exist, such as Little India, which is the focal point of Singapore's Indian community.

We travelled around Singapore by a variety of means, but the most impressive was their metro system. This small island's tiny rail transport system is surely a lesson to the rest of the world. It is the cleanest and most efficient I have ever experienced.

Singapore Zoo is also an exciting place to visit. At the zoo the animals are kept in spacious, landscaped ecological settings. We followed a programme whereby we attended areas where feeding, cleaning, or impromptu acts took place. We were so impressed with the zoo that we went back to see it all over again through a night safari. To see the animals, seemingly in their natural environment, at night was truly spectacular.

Another part of Singapore that impressed us was Sentosa Island, which is a kind of theme park. This is connected to the mainland by a variety of means. We chose to cross to the island via a glass cable car cabin. On the island there are a variety of theme areas to visit. Each area can be accessed in a number of ways. We used the monorail which continually circulates the island. There was too much for us to take in on a single day visit and, because of the limit on our time available, we had to leave many theme areas for another future visit. One of the attractions we really enjoyed was the musical fountains, which also included a laser show projected onto the cascading water.

A lasting impression we gained from Singapore was the politeness of all the people we met, a feeling of safety on the streets, cleanliness with an absence of graffiti and chewing gum, and a sense of national pride.

While staying in Singapore we took the opportunity to take in a coach tour of Malaysia, a country we had been told would impress us. The tour took in many of the traditional tourist spots, and we were certainly impressed by these. However, we were surprised at the many experiences of poor hygiene we were faced with. Perhaps we had been spoilt by the high standards we had found in Singapore!

A comical aspect of the tour of Malaysia was mealtimes. All meals encouraged a spirit of companionship between members of the tour. Dishes were put into the centre of a large table around which sat all the members of the tour. Everyone helped themselves to the food. So far so good! Unfortunately, Olivia and I were the only Europeans on the tour, and the serving and eating implements were chopsticks. We couldn't use them. Consequently, the deposit of a dish in the centre of the table was followed by a short burst of rapid clicking and, before we managed to get a few grains of rice on our plates, everything had gone.

Two young Chinese boys from Hong Kong, sitting on either side of us, clearly found it amusing that we couldn't use chopsticks. These charming little lads took to pointing to items on the dishes in the centre of the table and, if we nodded, they would deposit it on our plates, obviously proud to highlight our lack of dexterity.

One lad pointed to a small red item that looked to me like a European pickled pepper. He raised one eyebrow in question, I nodded, and he delivered the specimen straight into my mouth. His delight in seeing the shock on my face while trying to chew on a whole chilli was patently obvious. After this event, everyone took pity on us and we were supplied with a fork and spoon with each meal.

We flew on from Asia to Australia where I had to visit the offices of one of my publishers in Melbourne and lead a few seminars and deliver some lectures. The market potential for my books turned out to be too small for it to be worthwhile to adapt them especially for Australia, but I did identify some existing books by Australian authors that I could adapt for the larger European market.

While visiting the publishers in Melbourne I was taken to see Cook's cottage in a park. This was apparently the modest cottage that Cook's parents had built in 1755 on a "piece of waste ground" in the village of Great Ayton in Yorkshire. In a leaflet given to me, I read that the cottage had been put up for auction in 1933 purporting to be "Renowned as the home of Captain Cook's early days." The Australian state of Victoria bought the house and moved it to Melbourne, even transplanting the ivy that grew on the walls. And there it stood in this grand park.

I found this monument to Captain Cook a justifiable tourist attraction, honouring, in my view, an underrated explorer. However, there was one problem as I saw it. Cook could never have lived in the cottage. By the time

Cook's ageing parents had built the cottage, Cook was twenty-seven years of age and long gone from the area. He was already a Navy man and engaged in long voyages. In fact, as far as the records ascertain, Cook only ever travelled to Ayton once to see his parents there. But it was pleasing to see Australia was interested enough to want to remember the great British explorer. What a pity that the British were more inclined to sell their heritage! Or were the Australians conned?

Having made the long journey to Australia we decided to incorporate into the trip a sightseeing holiday and a visit to see my cousin and her husband. We planned to fly to Perth in South Western Australia and then, along with our relations, to drive up the west coast to as far north as time would allow.

Driving in Australia is an experience in itself, and is particularly relaxed when compared with the busy English roads. Our drive north followed the Great Highway that runs, roughly, parallel to the coast and, very roughly, circumvents right round Australia.

The road is generally amazingly straight, so that if you stand on the brow of a hill you can look north and south and see the road stretching straight in both directions. What is even more amazing is to be able to look in each direction and not see another vehicle in sight. What a contrast this was to the rat race we are used to on the M25 motorway that circumvents London, and where motorists dice with death on each and every journey, no matter what time of the day they travel. Probably the greatest danger we experienced

294

motoring in Australia was the possibility of kangaroos, emus or camels dashing in front of the car.

Another contrast with the M25 is that the side routes of the Great Highway are relatively narrow, even though they are linked to the major road around Australia. In many places the road is so narrow that when vehicles pass each other, each driver must steer the near side of their vehicle onto the compacted gravel of the hard shoulder to pass each other. This can be bad news for pedestrian backpackers! It also accounts for the many dead kangaroos and cattle seen alongside the road, the smell of which can be picked up well ahead of sight of them.

The road north was accompanied by an expanse of bush on either side. I had expected long rolling hills smothered with sheep, remembered from geography lessons when I was at school, but this was not so. The Australian bush is a parched, rough, red, uneven area that contrasts with the verdant English pastures. You need to be very careful where you put your feet, and even more careful where you squat when nature demands it. Snakes and spiders are in generous supply, and the ants are enormous. To us it seemed that every bush and shrub hid a threat of some sort or other. And there was always the intense heat and the flies.

We covered huge distances seeing little other than bushes, kangaroos, emus and occasionally wild camels for company. Houses and villages are few and far between. The only sign of habitation was seen in the occasional sign pointing the way up a gravel track leading to a "station". Sometimes these signs would be accompanied by a small bench offering farm produce for sale, with a tin (called an "honesty box") for the buyer to place their payment in for their purchases. I couldn't help thinking that in England, the farmer would come back and find his produce gone, and his money box also.

As we travelled north, every couple of hundred miles or so, we would come upon a roadhouse. These are places where we could get some petrol, and a bite to eat, if you could get the food into your mouth before it was invaded by flies. At one roadhouse we stopped by the petrol pump and waited to be served petrol. After about ten minutes wait I went inside the roadhouse to find no sign of life. But there was a hand rung bell to ring to summon service. In response to the loud clatter of the bell, the owner finally arrived. "Blimey, mate," he said, "You folks are really keeping me busy. You're the third customer today. Don't know how I'm going to get my chores done at this rate. Wotcha want, digger?" I said, "Some petrol will be helpful." "You'll have to wait while I go and turn the pump on." Even when he had done this, there was another wait while the pump got the pressure up to sufficient strength to deliver the petrol.

Having paid for the petrol we asked to use the toilets. "The dunnie's round the back," the guy informed us. We went round the back to the toilets, but they were locked. We went back round to the roadhouse, rang the hand-bell and explained to man the need to unlock the door. Off he went and came back with a key, which he gave to Olivia. But it was the key to the ladies and the men's toilet was locked also. Having spent forty minutes getting a fill up of petrol and visiting the toilet, we gave up and I used the ladies.

During a stop at another roadhouse, I visited the "dunnie". As I made to leave I spotted the ominous legs of the most enormous spider I had ever seen, seemingly beckoning me and daring me to come closer. I sidled out of the toilet along the wall, as far away from the spider as I could get. I relayed the terror of the toilets to my cousin, and she came with me to inspect the monster. She assured me that the spider was a "pussy cat" that would do me no harm, but warned me to be wary of a far smaller one with a red spot on its back that could hospitalise me.

In spite of the scary aspects of wild life in the bush, there was beauty within the harsh environment. There was birdlife of stunning beauty also. We saw a lovely green parrot that impressed us, but the Aussies referred to it by the unglamorous name of "Twenty-Eight", apparently because its call sounds like this number. And there were a variety of other exotic birds flying free, including the delicate pink and grey Galahs and many different species of Cockatoo, not to mention the Australian favourite, the Kookaburra with its distinct call. There were also spectacular butterflies with dazzling colours that hovered in the shrubs.

The flora of Western Australia is also quite spectacular, and during our travels we saw plenty growing in the wild in the bush that would enhance any British garden. We found the Banksia stunning with its spikes of flowers formed in dramatic cones. We also saw

297

lots of Kangaroo Paw, which is the floral emblem of Western Australia. One plant that particularly impressed us was seen in a gravel pit in open shrubland, and formed a ground level wreath-like shrub of yellow, pink and red flowers.

At a stop at one roadhouse we were welcomed by the customary, "G'day, mate", by the owner, an enormous man with a wide brimmed hat that not only protected his head, but also his shoulders from the intense heat. He warned us that a storm was brewing. This particular one turned out to be very different from the thunder and lightning and lashing rain we were used to in England. The bush storm arrived in great thunderous spirals of red dust that stung the eyes and invaded the mouth and nostrils, and coated shoes and clothing in a red film of dust.

Eventually, the rain did arrive in a heavy deluge, causing flash floods that suddenly turned gravel roads into instant quagmire, and changed dry river beds into fast flows that cut off roads. Fortunately, this storm lasted only a short while, its fury soon abated, and everywhere dried up quickly. We were soon able to continue our journey north. But the ferocity of the storm showed how an innocent-looking creek could quickly become a dangerous overflowing river, instead of providing essential water supplies.

We intended to travel on until we reached Darwin (which, as far as I can make out, Darwin himself never visited), but by the time we reached Broome, we needed a rest, and we decided to spend some time there before retracing our steps south. Whilst staying here we went on a camel safari. From the way one sways about on a camel's back, it is easy to see why they are called "ships of the desert".

In spite of my many visits to Australia as a seaman, it was not until I went to Broome that I met an Aborigine. Some of the Australians I talked to seemed prejudiced against the Aborigines, and talked disparagingly about them. I tried not to take a similar attitude, but my limited experience of the Aborigines I encountered in Broome left me feeling apprehensive in their presence. However, I found their artwork fascinating and many of their customs intriguing. The word "Aborigine" is Latin for "from the beginning". This seems an apt name for a people whose culture is possibly one of the oldest in the world.

We love the laid-back way of life in Australia and have now enjoyed several extended visits there, but my book work and family ties always call me back to Britain and Essex.

On the return journey to the UK from our first trip to Australia, we stopped over in Hong Kong, as previously mentioned, to enable me to meet representatives of my publishers in order to be taken to make goodwill visits to schools and colleges. Apart from the sad business of finding that two of my books had been plagiarised, our experience of Hong Kong was an introduction to yet another culture. We couldn't believe how so many people could be accommodated into so many high rise apartments.

We enjoyed a trip round Hong Kong Harbour in a motorised junk, but we were saddened to see so many people living crammed together in old rusting ships locked together in the harbour. We wonder today if this has changed and their lot improved since Hong Kong became part of China.

On a later trip to Australia, we took the opportunity to have a stop over in Thailand. I had read several accounts of the building of the infamous Burmese Railway, and we were able to take a train ride along this.

To get there we travelled along the River Kwai in a fast, long, narrow boat driven by an outboard motor, getting off at the famous bridge to board the train to cross the bridge and travel along the railway. We dismounted at an area where a group of wartime prisoners had been bricked up in a cave by their Japanese captors. We were told by our guide, "Mr Boone", these men had worked their way out of the cave tomb by tunnelling with their bare hands, and following subterranean tunnels to reach safety. He also told us that one year previously he had actually met one of the men who escaped. The man, who was then eighty-two years of age, was revisiting the site for the first time since his escape. On seeing this cave one could only wonder how his captors could have been so callous, and how anyone escaped such horror!

We were then taken to a military cemetery to some war graves. It was 22 July, my wife's birthday. As we were walking about in this place of pure peace, we came across the grave of a young soldier of nineteen who had died on 22 July 1943, the same day my wife was born. We were both deeply affected by the coincidence of this experience and the fact that we were visiting on the anniversary of the young man's death. A sad experience, but one that neither of us would have missed, nor will we ever forget it.

The latest experiences brought about by my books have led to an affinity with a small island and its people that I would not have thought possible. My most recent books, written for the Caribbean market, have necessitated several visits to Barbados. These visits, in order to be productive, have had to be for several weeks at a time. Each visit to the island has caused the place and the people to become endeared to us, and now they are really "under our skin".

On the first of these visits, we were to stay in Barbados for at least four weeks, and would need to visit the exam board and schools. I decided I would need to hire a car. As any visitor to Barbados will confirm, it is easy to spot a tourist because their vehicles have a distinguishing type of number plate. I wanted to avoid this recognition and draw less attention from potential thieves (I had been warned about this by locals).

I negotiated a "special deal" with a local guy. I hired his "best" car at a special rate, with normal local plates. It was a reasonable car by local standards, although I could have bought two of them at home for the cost of the hire. It was disconcerting to be able to see the road through the floor in places and, when it was raining, you had to be careful where to position things to avoid them getting wet.

I asked the guy what we should do if the car broke down. He seemed shocked that I should even contemplate this happening, but said, "Just phone me on this number. If I'm not there, I'm somewhere else." This sums up the kind of lingo you need to take on board when dealing with Bajans. Another terminology we had to get used to was, "I go to come back." This basically means, "I'm going now, but I will see you later." But, like all colloquialisms, there are a variety of other interpretations.

Driving in Barbados is part of a different world. Well, certainly different from my world! Very few people drive fast in Barbados, partly because a lot of the roads are so bad. The faster you drive the more teeth you are likely to knock out. Even the main highways (their equivalent of a motorway) contain potholes that can do serious damage to both the car and the driver. But at least you can tell that they drive on the left! In some places I have visited the driving is so chaotic it is difficult to be sure which side of the road they drive.

Quite apart from the poor condition of the roads, driving is generally slow and relaxed, reflecting the nature of most Bajans. It's the tourists you need to be wary of, especially during "happy hour". I once sat in a traffic queue whilst two taxi drivers stopped to talk to each other through their open car windows. The drivers in both directions in the queue sat patiently, without hitting the horn, until the men finished their chat and drove on, allowing traffic to flow again. This would have been an excuse for a patch of road rage at home!

302

There is an exception to the relaxed driver in Barbados, and these are the ZR drivers. ZRs are a kind of minibus-come-people carrier. They are used to provide a service that is halfway between a taxi and a bus. The rules of the game are that you can flag down a ZR at any place on their route, and join the sweating crowd inside. For $1.50 (Bajan), you can go as far as you want along its route. They are the exception to the rule for Bajan drivers because they drive at breakneck speed, rarely give any signals, stop suddenly to pick up customers, blast everyone near with crescendo music, and have their hand permanently on the horn. Hmm, sounds a bit like the M25 at home!

There are many Rastafarians, or "Rastas", on Barbados. When we first met them around the island we were nervous of them, with their dreadlocks and brightly knitted hats, and looking rather out of place. But, as we got used to them, we found them fine to get on with and nothing like as fierce as we imagined they might be.

It seems that the origin of the Rasta is as colourful as their appearance. The Emperor of Ethiopia, Haile Selase, had paid a visit to Jamaica in his youth, when he was known as "Ras Tafari". He became a bit of a cult figure in Jamaica and the wider Caribbean with his dreadlocks, and his followers became known as Rastafarians or Rasta.

At the end of one tiring day of visiting schools and meeting teachers, we visited Oistins Fish Fry, a popular tourist food and music venue, to search for food and drink. On a Friday night the area would be teeming

303

with overdressed tourists, but now, midweek, we had it much to ourselves. Everything was much the same as Friday night, except that the crowds were not there, which suited us fine.

First we went to a rum shack to collect drinks to take to the eating area. I ordered a quart of rum, a bottle of coke, glasses and a bowl of ice. "You want dark rum or light rum, man," the guy asked. "Dark rum," I replied. "Ain't got no dark rum," he said, "Got plenty light rum." Bingo, we had a deal, and I was beginning to cotton on to the delightful Bajan communication system.

We walked with the drinks across the road to the eating area where several large barbeques blazed away. "Watcha got?" I enquired in my newly acquired Bajan lingo. "Them's dolphin steaks. But not the "Flipper" dolphin you think, man. This mighty good stuff. Came in just an hour ago." This boast was probably quite true because nearby a woman was cleaning and filleting fish and cutting it into steaks. With the dolphin we had cooked breadfruit and plantain, neither of which we had eaten before. We also tried flying fish that I had not realised could taste so good.

The little Bajan villages of brightly coloured chattel houses are very pretty. These tiny homes are perched on stilts; I assumed this was to encourage air to flow underneath, but it may have also been to discourage easy access for wildlife. However, nothing seemed to keep out the cockroaches and mosquitoes.

Many houses had rusting cars in their gardens, some of which were now inhabited by chickens that seemed to roam with no apparent ownership. In spite of their tiny proportions, many of the chattel houses were brightly painted in proud traditional Bajan style. In contrast to my expectations, young teenagers emerged immaculately dressed in school uniforms that would have been complimentary to the best private schools in Britain.

I visited several secondary schools as part of a public relations exercise to promote my books, and also to become familiar with local strategies used in teaching. The physical structure of the school buildings is different from British schools in that they have many large openings to allow the breeze to flow through, but other features were similar — morning assemblies, and seats outside the headteacher's office to accommodate scallywags.

I was for some reason disappointed to find punishment desks outside of the headteacher's office, probably because out on the streets I found pupils in school uniform extraordinarily polite when compared with many British school teenagers. At the bus stop I was frequently and freely greeted with, "Good morning, Sir," or, "We hope you are having a nice time in Barbados." They obviously recognised me as a tourist!

It wasn't all work for me in Barbados. What is the point of going to paradise and not seeing what's there? We visited the typical tourist spots, which are mainly located on the west coast. One morning we were walking along a particularly beautiful and relatively empty beach we liked, when we passed a famous British

305

celebrity walking in the opposite direction, looking pretty miserable it seemed. We had no intention of invading his privacy, or even showing recognition, because we know many "stars" do not like this. But we politely said, "Good morning" which was completely ignored, and he went on his morose way.

One week later, we read an article in one of the English tabloids written by this man. In it our celebrity was revelling in the fact that he had just returned from two weeks in Barbados. The essence of the article was to justify spending £10,000 for a fortnight in Barbados (albeit flying by Concord), because his tough lifestyle drained him so much. I'm sure that the British public must have felt very sorry for him, and suitably impressed by his ability to spend more on a two week holiday than many of them would earn in a whole year. For me, it seemed ironic that he would pay so much to walk on the same beach that we were on at a tiny fraction of the cost. Quite apart from this, he did not look as if he was enjoying his holiday anyway.

Part of the difference in cost, apart from flying by Concord, is of course due to the difference in accommodation. He was clearly staying in a swish hotel, where he would have minimal exposure to local culture. We prefer to be away from the pristine hotels, mixing more with the locals, who are a delight to know. Away from the tourist centres there are poorly surfaced lanes, abounded by the brightly coloured chattel houses described earlier. This is the real Barbados. Many of the homes appear unfinished concoctions of scrap lumber, coral blocks, and corrugated iron, although invariably outrageously brightly painted.

On the streets, road signs appear haphazardly hung askew, and standpipes are still a common feature in some areas. Chickens and dogs wander loose with no apparent home. But civility is ever present. Stop at crossroads to ask for directions, and you are immediately surrounded by people from a nearby rum shack, competing with each other to be the one to give advice and send you in the right direction.

Although the west coast, with its palm fringed beaches and the gentle Caribbean sea, is the most popular with tourists, we have a preference for the quieter east coast. The east coast combines gentle hills, coconut groves and banana plantations, and dramatic cliffs facing the wild Atlantic Ocean. This side of the island is less suitable for swimming because the sea tends to be rough and less safe than the west coast. But it is ideal for windsurfers, and offers more solitude for those looking for space away from the normal tourists.

All around Barbados, the brilliant white sand is reflected in the bright turquoise of the sea. While many countries suffer from litter of discarded plastic bottles, this is not the case in Barbados. Why? Because the country puts a surcharge on drinks sold in this type of container, and collectors are offered a refund when they are handed in at collection points. Tourists, of course, still throw their bottles where they wish, but the locals quickly collect them. Consequently you are more likely to find coconuts on the beaches than plastic bottles because, even when bottles are discarded, there are plenty of people ready to collect them and obtain the refund.

On the quieter beaches you can sit and watch young men pulling fish from the surf, waist deep in the water, armed only with a throwing net and a basket to carry away their bounty. These opportunist fishermen fillet the catch on the spot and sell it to you very cheaply, and they will throw in a prepared freshly cut coconut free. All this is of no interest to tourists from hotels, of course, but those, like us, who were self-catering snapped up their offerings.

My favourite snack food in Barbados is a roti. The roti originates from India, but Barbados has its own distinct versions. It can best be described as a flat, thin, round water and flour pastry outer casing, with a curry type filling that is folded into a semi-circular package and cooked. The roti is really the outer casing although most people refer to a roti as the complete package. The curry filling can be made with any kind of meat, such as chicken, beef, shrimp, etc. A more exotic roti has a filling made from lamb — not lamb as from sheep, but a shellfish taken from the Conche.

"Happy Hour" is an important part of the Bajan day. It is the time when drinks are half price. Bars vary in the length of their happy hour, and it often extends to two hours. They also vary in the time they have happy hour. So, you can go to one place and enjoy happy hour and then go on to another place and do the whole thing again, so long as you can stand up long enough, and walk from one bar to another.

Our earliest experience of happy hour was to cause us some difficulty. We drove up the west coast to a beachside bar to take advantage of happy hour, and to watch the sunset. Bear in mind that Olivia doesn't touch alcohol! My strategy was to order two rum and cokes for myself, and two non-alcoholic coconut punches for Olivia. The theory being that two rum and cokes of their generous measures would last me well beyond their happy hour, and still allow me to drive home to our lodgings.

Unfortunately, I had miscalculated the happy hour notice to mean half-price drinks. Wrong! In this place it meant two for the price of one. So I had four rum and cokes lined up, a beautiful palm-shaded beach, a stunning sunset, and wobbly legs after three of the rum and cokes. Fortunately, Olivia is an excellent driver and we made it safely back to our temporary home.

Our second experience of happy hour wasn't much better. Armed with the knowledge of our first happy hour in Barbados, we decided for our next session, at lunchtime, we would walk to a bar near our lodgings. This was another lovely place with the bar almost on the white sand. Gently does it! I order one rum punch (rum and coconut), and non-alcoholic punch for Olivia. Two of each arrived — safe so far. The rum punch tasted so nice that I suggested to Olivia that she really must try one of my rum punches. I didn't realise the powerful effect alcohol can have on someone who abstains. I knew we were in trouble when she slid off the bar stool half way through the drink, and I wasn't much better. On this occasion we had to walk home in the intense heat of the midday sun, helping each other along. We certainly treated Bajan hospitality more carefully from then on, and we no longer disgraced the British reputation.

As previously mentioned, and as you will have gathered, I have grown to love Barbados and its people, but I suspect I have a different perspective from the normal tourist. I assume this has developed from several long-term visits where we have concentrated our time on living and working with the local residents. Even so, after an extended time in the sticky and hot air we begin to yearn for a change. I spoke to a Canadian who had settled there. "After a while," he said, "you need air, you need to fly away, to regain the longing for the beauty of the place. Once a year I fly back to Canada, just to see the snow and feel the crisp air. It's crazy, isn't it?" But there is no doubt about the allure of the island that draws people back time and again. In my case, work also draws me back, and the taxman generously assists!

All of the experiences related in this final chapter have happened because of my writing, so I have every reason to be thankful for my books. When I was young I can vividly remember an adult loaning me a book. It was probably the most expensive book I had ever had my hands on at that time. When I returned it, I now realise, it must have been a bit dog-eared. In those days I didn't think about things like bookmarks. I just folded over a corner of the page to mark the place I had reached. Fortunately, the lender was very tolerant and he only said to me, "Alan, be kind to books and they will be good to you." Little did this person realise how true these words would turn out to be. How apt his advice has been — books have certainly been good to me.

EPILOGUE

In parts of this book I have related the extensive travels I have enjoyed around the world, either through my time in the Merchant Navy or as a result of my writing. Whatever the reason for my travelling, my Essex roots have always remained uppermost in my mind, and it has been to Essex that I have always returned.

Similarly, in places I have recounted my many academic achievements, in spite of failing that so very important Eleven-Plus exam at a young age. I often wonder how many others of my generation were similarly hindered and limited by this flawed assessment of their academic ability. In this respect, I never forget the times when I had no qualifications, nor the desperation and lack of self-esteem I felt while unemployed.

Although this book has my personal experiences as its backbone, the reader should look upon it as a reflection of what was taking place in Essex during the period covered by the book: the exodus of so many Londoners escaping our war torn capital; the bygone age of hop picking, so popular with Londoner and Essex families; the flawed education system that

312

existed; the importance of Tilbury Docks at that time, not only to the local economy but also to the country; and, of course, the disastrous floods that ravaged Essex in 1953.

I have often been asked how I arrived at the point in my life that I have now reached. Well, it has been a long, hard, and colourful road from my hop picking beginnings to the peak of academic achievement. After describing my life to others, the comment has frequently been, "You really should put it in a book." I made many attempts to make inroads into writing this book, but the difference in style required when compared with my academic books often seemed too great.

The general image of an author is that their best work is done lying on their backs by the pool, with a drink in their hand, contemplating their navel and waiting for inspiration to hit them. That may be the case for some authors, but it is certainly not what happens with me. Perhaps it is because of the academic nature of the work I normally do. I have now published more than thirty books with seven different publishers, and these have all involved long, hard slogs and meticulous planning, many re-writes, and long periods of solitude.

There are times of the day when I seem to work best, and this often results in working very unsociable hours. For example, I seem to work best in the evening, often getting into full flow in the late hours, and then working into the early hours of the morning, trying to exploit good progress to the full before it evaporates.

The problem with writing a book like this one is that, as you put your thoughts down on paper, so many other things and people you have known who have influenced you come to mind. And often words cannot recapture their effect on your development: the paupers in Naples offering their sisters for sex; the maimed beggars in Aden pleading for a pittance from makeshift roller boards; the begging woman in Crete who threw my money back in my face because she was so sure I could afford more.

This book has been very different from my many others. Here I have been a novice again, struggling to express what I want to say in a way that will be of interest to others, and hoping to make them laugh along the way. I have nibbled away at it over a number of years, hoping that some publisher would recognise it as more than an interesting portrayal of my life, but also part of a historical record of relatively recent times.

The fact that you are reading this means I have eventually completed the task, and that a publisher has accepted it. I hope that you have found the reading interesting, and I also hope that it may give encouragement to other "school failures" to try again — it's never too late!

Also available in ISIS Large Print:

Growing up in Sussex

Gerry Wells

Rescued by Father, probably startled from his newspaper, I was handed dripping and yelling over the fence to be sorted out by Mother who wouldn't have been amused. A second baptism perhaps, just to make sure.

This compelling memoir starts with a boy's journey through the early years of the 1930s — days of the rag and bone man, street lamplighters and in the background, Hitler. Then life gets real, at school where cane and cricket bat rule and even more real with army call-up and training.

In 1944/45 comes the crunch of combat in Operation Overlord. And after all that, with his ears still ringing a bit, comes the blessed call of demob and a taste of new delights, finding a woman daft enough to marry him before settling near his work on a farm to start his life as a man.

ISBN 978-0-7531-9540-6 (hb)
ISBN 978-0-7531-9541-3 (pb)

Suburban Boy

Adrian Bristow

It was while we lived in Herbert Road that I acquired my toy box . . . It was quite large enough for me to climb into and it became by turns a boat, a cave or a house, according to which story or character was exercising my imagination at the time.

Suburban Boy is the charming story of a bygone era, of a boy who grew up in south-east London in the 1930s. Adrian Bristow came from that great unsung mass — the lower middle-class. He grew up in the years before the war, which saw the Depression, the Abdication, the rise of Hitler and the coming of war. It was also a time of rising standards of living, burgeoning home ownership, social mobility and the emergence of first-generation graduates. It was a time when there was respect for authority and a strong consciousness of nation and empire.

ISBN 978-0-7531-9538-3 (hb)
ISBN 978-0-7531-9539-0 (pb)

In the Shelter of Each Other

Jack Maddox

I prattled away and enthused and extolled the wonders of the library and this new experience all the way home. It changed my life, for it was a new interest with an infinite capability for progression and pleasure.

Liverpool, April 1932. England is out of work. The mills are silent, and in the river, ships are rusting at anchor. The king is ageing and his successor remains unmarried. In Germany Adolf Hitler has come to power and begun reclaiming lost territories.

It is the wrong time and place to arrive in the world, but Jack appears all the same. A childhood spent in a bustling dockside pub in the roughest, toughest part of the city and an early introduction to the school of hard knocks. Lawless, tribal and violent, but also exciting, humorous and generous. Bonded by poverty, few had much, but nobody died alone.

ISBN 978-0-7531-9536-9 (hb)
ISBN 978-0-7531-9537-6 (pb)

Does He Speak Welsh?

John Scott

Suddenly they were all talking about me. Then came the phrase that I would come to hear so often that it became burned into my soul, "Ydy e'n siarad Cymraeg?" (Does he speak Welsh?)

In this delightful, childhood memoir the author takes us back to the time when he was evacuated from wartime Newcastle, with his mother, to stay with an elderly aunt in Wales. It was a time when the local people all conversed fluently in their own native tongue, and the diverse characters he met were a fascination for him. Not least, was his Uncle Bob the local baker who introduced him to the mysteries of bread-making.

A year or so later, mother and son left the safe, slow lifestyle of seaside Pwllheli, and its surrounding mountainous countryside, to rejoin his father in Newcastle.

ISBN 978-0-7531-8400-4 (hb)
ISBN 978-0-7531-8401-1 (pb)